W9-AQI-870

NOBODY'S BABY

NOBODY'S BABY

A Survival Guide to Politics

Sheila Copps

DENEAU

Deneau Publishers & Company Ltd.
760 Bathurst Street
Toronto, Ontario
M5S 2R6

© 1986 Sheila Copps
Printed in Canada

This book has been published with the assistance of the Canada Council
and Ontario Arts Council under their block grant programmes.

Canadian Cataloguing in Publication Data

Copps, Sheila, 1952–
  Nobody's baby: a survival guide to politics

ISBN 0-88879-135-6

1. Copps, Sheila, 1952– . 2. Women in politics —
Canada. 3. Women legislators — Canada — Biography.
4. Ontario Liberal Party. 5. Ontario – Politics and
government — 1943– *. 6. Canada — Politics and
government — 1984– *. I. Title.

FC631.C66A3 1986   328.71'092'4   C86-094142-6
F1034.3.C66A3 1986

To my husband, Ric, for sharing my choices. To my parents, Vic and Gerry, for showing me choices by example. To my sisters, Mary and Brenda, and brother Kevin, for sticking together regardless of choices.

Contents

PREFACE

When I was asked to write a book about women and politics, my first response was a resounding "No!". Not another Liberal writing a book! But as any politician should know, never say never. I went home and mulled it over, wondering whether I had anything to say that might be worth listening to. Then I realized if there is one message that women in politics must send, it is that there simply aren't enough of us in the fray to make our voices heard. If this book prompts one fence-sitter to get involved, if it encourages one woman to become a candidate, then it will have been a success.

Political life is often shrouded in myths, hyped by the media and inaccessible to the people. This book is my attempt to throw off that shroud, to pull back the curtains and to show you the ups and downs of a life that can be both stimulating and frustrating. There are thousands of Canadians who watch question-period antics on the nightly news and think that's all there is to our political process. They lose sight of the fact that in a democracy, the process reflects the involvement of people like you and me; ordinary people who feel we might not have all the answers but we certainly know what questions should be asked. No party and no politician has all the answers. What we need to stimulate new ideas is the involvement of more people at the grass roots level. The steelworker in Hamilton has as much stake in the future of our country as the businessman on Bay Street. But as long as the steelworker stays on the periphery, allowing other people to make the political decisions affecting our lives, he or she will never help shape a people's Canada.

And so it is for women. As long as we are content to sit on the sidelines and serve the coffee while our men run the country, we will be left out when it comes to positive social change. I'm talking about power. Not power for the sake of self-aggrandizement, but power that can shape priorities for women, for families, for the real future of our country.

Women won't want to attain that power in an isolationist fashion. We aren't out to threaten, intimidate or annihilate men. But what we do want is a chance to set the priorities that flow from power. We want to work together with men; we want to be an equal, viable and aggressive part of the process.

The slogan says, "We've come a long way, baby". And we have. In my mother's day, there was only one role, as a wife and mother. Now we have choices. Difficult, trying choices but choices nonetheless. I am asking the women of our country to choose change; change through a political process that will only be real when it reflects the reality of the majority of Canadians, our women.

ACKNOWLEDGMENTS

To Joyce Wayne, for believing in this book. To Danielle May, for picking up the pieces. To Molly Wolf, for establishing order from chaos.

1

The Challenge of Chance

Rule 1: When opportunity knocks the timing is always right

Almost ten years ago, I was sitting at my desk at the Hamilton *Spectator*. It was 10 pm and my first day on the job as a newspaper reporter. The phone rang. A strange man said hello and introduced himself as the president of the Hamilton Centre Liberal Association. He said he wanted me to run as a candidate in the provincial election campaign, already in progress. My first reaction was to burst out laughing. "You've got to be crazy. No one in their right mind would vote for me," I said. I thought that my age, 24, my inexperience and my sex combined to make me a losing candidate, a typical sacrificial lamb. He insisted, claiming that the organization had plenty of money, energy and volunteers. All they were lacking was a candidate.

Even though I thought I was unelectable, I decided to go ahead. In a sense, I had nothing to lose. No family, no mortgage, no financial responsibilities. With 23 days left in the campaign, I became the Liberal candidate in a riding which had not been Liberal since 1934.

Before I left the *Spectator*, the managing editor warned, "Sheila, you'll be slaughtered, they're using you. All they want is your name." His analysis was partly true; my father had been a popular mayor in our city for almost fourteen years and his name was the only reason I was approached. But there's nothing like another's pessimism to get my Irish up.

When I entered the race, I quickly learned a rule which I've never forgotten: *don't count on the party to deliver. The candidate is the bottom line.* Once the writ is issued (i.e. when the election is called), it's every one for him or herself in the scramble for workers, ideas, money and organization. In the case of Hamilton Centre, I learned that my information was wrong. We had no money, no people and no organization. All we had was a candidate. The situation was so bad that the previous Liberal candidate was working for the Tories and the riding association was in receivership.

What we lacked in expertise, we made up for in energy. Since the campaign period was short, we would start at 6 am visiting steel factories. Then I would go door to door all day and wind up with an evening "flying squad." Since we needed every vote we could get, we would try to bring out every last worker in the evenings. With squads of 20 or 30, we would divide up the streets. Each phalanx would swoop down on its appointed route, complete with piped-in music, the candidate (me) and any other notable political figure we could muster. The federal cabinet minister, John Munro, who had been instrumental in encouraging me to run, would often join. We would literally run from street to street, to make sure that time was spent with each of the groups to maintain a strong candidate presence. Indeed, it was from John that we borrowed the political blitz techniques which had worked so well for him for 25 years.

To show how little I knew about the political process, the night before our nomination papers were due we had regrouped, as usual, at our headquarters to discuss our progress. At about 11 pm, some bright soul asked where our nomination papers were. My reply: "What are nomination papers?" I soon discovered that, notwithstanding all our efforts to date, if we could not muster 100 signatures by noon the following day, my candidacy would be null and void. Where do you find 100 people at midnight? That's right; at the tavern. A team of supporters spent the next hour scouring the local pubs asking for volunteers to sign my nomination papers. The following morning at 6 am I was standing at factory gates asking local workers not only to vote for me, but to get me nominated. We got our names in by noon, almost 200 of them; we needed the extras to make up for such signatories as Godzilla (current address, planet of the apes).

Once the nomination papers were in, I could breathe a sigh of relief and carry on with the task at hand — winning a seat for the Liberals in a riding that had been NDP for sixteen years. I was scared stiff. I wondered whether I knew enough about the issues, whether people would accept a 24-year-old political novice. I had 23 days to learn all the ropes, from giving a speech to mainstreeting. Would I cut the mustard?

As a born ham, I had no problem with public speaking. As a student, I had always been interested in languages and took great joy in speaking to constituents in their own language. Hamilton Centre is a working-class riding with strong ethnic ties. Speaking Italian was an immense help to me, since the largest proportion of immigrants were Italian. However, I didn't stop at the languages I knew. If I was going to a Polish picnic or a Hungarian dance, I always tried to work a few words in the native language into my speech. That desire to speak the language actually resulted in one of the most embarrassing moments in my political career. The east end of Hamilton has a large Serbo-Croatian community. They share a common language but have distinct religious, cultural and political backgrounds. The political division between Serbians and Croatians exists even in Canada. One weekend I visited a Croatian dance on the Saturday night and a Serbian picnic the following day. At the Croatian dance, I learned to stumble through the phrase *dobar dan hrvati*, which, my hosts assured me, meant "good afternoon people." In fact, the literal translation is "good afternoon Croatian people." But I didn't know that when, the next day, I arrived at the Serbian picnic. I said "dobar dan hrvati" and 600 potential voters visibly recoiled in horror. I had just told a group of Serbians "good afternoon, Croatians" — the ultimate insult. My Serbian hosts were quick to hustle me off the stage and try to make amends. I didn't really understand their language, they explained. Later, a husky young Serbian man approached me and said I should thank my stars that I was a woman. Otherwise, I would have been taken out in the alley and assaulted.

Since I subsequently lost the election by fourteen votes, the Croatian caper was costly.

Another recurring fear for any new politician is whether you can master all the issues. Since I had been nominated long after the election was called, I didn't have time to read up on every aspect of Liberal party policy. My naiveté really came to the fore when Liberal leader Dr. Stuart Smith joined me in an all-party debate at one of the local high schools. The Liberals were floundering badly, and Stuart was trying to show the provincial media that he had a crop of bright new candidates. Ian Deans represented the NDP at the debate along with the incumbent NDP member, Mike Davison, whom I was trying to unseat. The Tories had their representatives there too, but the real fight was between the Liberals and the NDP. I was nervous, wondering how I would cope with the additional publicity of Stuart's presence.

Someone in the audience asked me a question about a newly-announced job creation programme for young people. Mustering up as much courage as I could, I explained that the programme would provide funding for any young person who wanted to set up a business. For some inexplicable reason, I began talking about setting up a fish-and-chip shop. The NDP smelled blood. One student, obviously a plant, jumped up and said he didn't go to school for thirteen years to run a fish-and-chip shop. Ian Deans came down hard on my *faux pas*. I countered by trying to joke that a native of the British Isles like Ian should recognize the benefits of the family fish-and-chip operation. Stuart defended me, but the damage was done. The next day the headlines blared across Ontario: Candidate gets leader into frying pan.

We huddled in the headquarters, trying to assess the damage. Then we agreed that the best defence is a good offence. I managed to track down a couple who lived in the riding and owned a fish-and-chip store that was on the verge of bankruptcy. The couple said the Liberal small business programme would mean the survival of their operation. We called a press conference at the fish-and-chip store so we could have the last word. Our fish-and-chip fry dominated the local news for three days, so we accomplished our objective — getting my name out to the public.

One thing surprised me; most people weren't interested in talking about major policy. They wanted to know the candidate, to say hello and express their hopes or concerns. Just having a chance to meet the candidate personally seemed to satisfy most voters.

The campaign sped by. It was the fastest 23 days in my life. We worked all day, every day, right up to polling day. There wasn't an unturned stone left anywhere. In fact, our last campaign act

17

was to meet the steel company workers coming in on the 11 pm shift the night before the election.

On E-day (election day) I got up bright and early and spent the day on the phones, talking to known Liberal supporters and urging them to get out and vote. In almost any local or provincial election, especially in urban areas, more people stay home than vote. And those stay-at-homes can make or break a candidate.

I recall talking to one young voter a few minutes before the polls closed. He admitted to being a Liberal but felt his vote really didn't mean that much. He didn't think he would go to the polls. I cajoled, begged, persuaded, pleaded and encouraged, all to no avail. He thought his vote was just one out of thousands and it wasn't worth the bother.

I remembered him a few hours later as the results came in. The tally between the New Democratic incumbent and me seesawed back and forth all night. Finally, the unofficial tally was in; I had lost the election by fifteen votes. Fifteen, of the more than 20,000 who cast their ballots in the election. I couldn't cry, I couldn't laugh, I couldn't look back. In 23 days, our team had put out every last ounce of possible energy but we quickly learned another lesson: *Never regret your losses; failure is honourable too.* I'd gotten my feet wet, indeed I'd undergone total immersion — but success or failure is a long-term thing.

Because of the closeness of the race, there was a recount. I took the view that I had already lost, and that any reversal of that fate would be a miracle. The recount confirmed our loss. I had come within fifteen votes of being the member of the provincial Parliament for Hamilton Centre, and failed. But the failure was the best thing that ever happened to me. Politically speaking, of course.

2

Interlude

Rule 2: Never fear failure

For too long, and for many reasons, women have allowed our cities, provinces and country to be governed almost solely by men. The reasons are legion, and a sociologist or political scientist could analyze them far more ably than I. Some are historical; we only got the vote in 1918. Likewise, economic barriers have held women back. Before the introduction of election financing laws (which still don't exist in many elections) the nomination often went to the one who could afford to mount the most impressive (read expensive) campaign for it. And whether we like to admit it or not, most women with families still have the primary responsibility for child rearing. Obviously, all of these factors combine to ensure, deliberately or not, that most of our democratic institutions are dominated by men.

My views may be heretical but I believe that the *single biggest factor holding women back is the fear of failure.*

We are afraid of making speeches, afraid of crossing swords with men in the boy's club atmosphere that typifies our halls of power. We are afraid of making fools of ourselves. This shouldn't be surprising. As children and adolescents, we are still not confronted with the kind of competition that typifies growing up in a man's world.

Take our high school system. Boys get out there on the football field and "fight, fight, fight," while we stand on the sidelines in cute little knee-freezing cheerleader outfits, waving our pompoms. Hardly the best way to learn to compete. So when can we learn to hold our own? How can we discover when to go forward, when to hold back, when to accept defeat, when to push for a win? When do we have a chance to experience the hurt of failure, and to bounce back?

I remember as a teenager attending high school dances. The girls would cluster in one half of the gymnasium and the boys would hold up the wall at the other end. A boy would take that long trek across the floor to ask a girl to dance. And if that girl said no, that long, lonely, rejected walk back was the height of humiliation. But that humiliation set the ground for success. Boys learn this sort of failure from a very early age. Failure is painful, but they develop ways of coping with it. Girls, on the other hand, are traditionally sheltered, exposed neither to the hurt nor the success.

I remember as a university student expressing my interest in becoming a lawyer. That is, until a male friend asked me why would I enter law school, displacing some poor young man who would have to support a family through his career. At the time, I silently nodded agreement.

Consider also the ultimate rite of passage. At her wedding ceremony, traditionally the most important day in her life, the bride is expected to remain modestly silent while her spouse, father and uncles make all the speeches.

Given then that women are traditionally sheltered in their formative years, is it then so surprising that on the average only 10 per cent of members of Parliament are female? We have had little practice at taking risks, we are brought up to be cautious and careful. Never be afraid to take the chance. Try for the school board position. Get involved in your local hospital board. Speak out on community issues. You may fall flat on your face but learning to fail is as important as learning to succeed.

I failed in 1977. I spent the next four years learning my lesson. There I was, out of a job, defeated in my first election, and faced with the challenge of turning that failure into success. I didn't dwell on the failure. In fact, I considered it a success. Although I had not succeeded in my first attempt at the polls, I had begun to understand the process, and I knew that if I had the courage to stick it out, the sky was the limit.

Our provincial leader, Stuart Smith, represented the riding of Hamilton West, next to the Hamilton Centre riding on which I had set my sights. He needed an assistant in his riding and I needed a job. It was the perfect political marriage. I spent four years learning the ropes of government by day and politics by night. A constituency assistant is in many ways closer to the people than a politician. You are the front line. When people call their member of Parliament to complain, chances are the politician may never personally speak to them. They do talk, however, to the assistant who can get involved in things as simple as tracking down a cheque or as complicated as helping to trace a kidnapped child.

You discover where the law works and where it fails in its primary objective: to help ordinary people live a better life. I saw the horrors of unworkable legislation and the joys of good laws. Above all, I learned how laws had a real and direct effect on the daily lives of working Canadians.

By day, I worked to cut through the red tape of government; by night I worked in the community. The better I knew my community, the more I could reasonably expect to reflect community concerns if I were elected to office. The more I knew the people of Hamilton, the greater chance I had to earn their support, or (at worst) their neutrality. Politically speaking, it's best if they vote for you but it's not bad if they don't vote against you and sit the election out.

The riding of Hamilton Centre had been dominated by the New Democratic Party for two decades. Most card-carrying New Democrats are committed to the principles of democratic socialism and would sooner be caught dead than working in an election for a Liberal. However, because of my involvement at the community level, I came to know many of the key players. While I never thought that they would actually support me, I did hope that because of our friendship, they might campaign more actively in other ridings than in mine.

In the working-class riding of Hamilton Centre, I needed that neutrality to beat out an incumbent whose family had held the riding for almost 20 years. The incumbent, Michael Davison, had succeeded his father as NDP member in 1975. Through his 1977 victory against me, he had more time to solidify his support. By 1981 we were facing an incumbent with six years experience in the Ontario legislature. However, we had also had the advantage of a four-year non-stop campaign in the community. While the member was in the legislature, I was working in the constituency.

Not only was I active in the office of Stuart Smith, but I got involved in many community issues affecting the east end of Hamilton. I worked with a group opposing the construction of an expressway. I helped organize opposition to the closing of a school in the area's Beach Boulevard community. I attended coffee parties in the homes of constituents who invited their neighbors for coffee and conversation with the future Liberal candidate. The conversations didn't always touch on provincial politics. I remember one discussion in the home of an Italian resident who was a great fan of Mussolini. One of his neighbors despised *Il Duce* and the two men ended up in a fist fight, one screaming his disapproval of

Mussolini and the other bellowing his support. I sat at the dining room table, nursing an espresso; beginning to understand how seriously politics is taken in some parts of the world.

We built the organization and planned for an early nomination. I was actually nominated almost two years before the 1981 election. The nomination was uncontested because I had shown early that I was prepared to work for four years to build a winning team.

Four years on the hustings is a long time. But when the next election was called, we were ready. This time, the campaign team had the nomination papers in order, the election strategy planned and the community support built up. The campaign was well organized and the people in it were committed, not only to my victory, but to the cause of liberalism.

The nomination was uncontested and I won the election against *the same incumbent* by almost 3,000. I had my foot in the door at last.

3

Out of the Kitchen

Rule 3: You can stand the heat

One of the few consolations of spending 40 years in opposition is that you learn how to throw great parties. The night of the election, we had one. Although I had won in Hamilton Centre, the Liberals were once again in opposition facing a majority Conservative government. Nonetheless, we celebrated by staying up all night, and returned to the factory gates the following morning to thank the workers. The dozen or so who had been together through the good and bad times of the past four years had breakfast together and then we went our separate ways. I went back to my apartment, where I waited for a telephone call from the CBC news in Toronto about the election results.

My emotions were mixed. While I was obviously on a high of election victory, I was feeling another emotion which was very unlike me: fear. Some women liken the response to postpartum depression. I had carried this goal, this "baby" around with me for four years, and now that I had made it, I was scared stiff. Like many people, I had only seen provincial politicians on television, on the 30-second clip, where they sometimes look intelligent and as if they know what they are talking about. I wondered whether

I could measure up, and once again I feared making a fool of myself in a man's world.

Before I went to Queen's Park, I took my mother aside. (I would have gone to my father for advice but he was too ill to offer any.) My mother is a first-rate political tuning fork. Her advice: "Sheila, whatever you do, don't heckle. I can't stand watching those politicians yelling and screaming at each other and getting paid for it." As any good daughter, I took my mother's advice under consideration, and quickly discarded it.

Some few weeks into the session, the Conservative housing minister was being questioned about the high price of houses in Metro Toronto. He kept saying that it was all the fault of those nasty Liberals in Ottawa. A number of us were heckling, but since I was the only woman in the Liberal party, my voice tended to pierce through the din. I yelled, "Abolish the ministry if you can't do anything." The minister stopped in his place, peered over at me and said, "If the member for Hamilton Centre would take up the habit of listening, she would be okay in this legislature. She should not try to perform like the former member for St. George, who got into the habit of yelling and shouting and made little or no sense. The member for Hamilton Centre is following very adequately in her footsteps. The only thing I would say to the member for Hamilton Centre is she is better looking than the former member for St. George." The minister was comparing me to outgoing Liberal member Margaret Campbell, who retired from politics at age 68. A government backbencher added insult to injury by shouting, "Go back to the kitchen."

Since this was my first experience with chauvinism in the House, I wanted to be cautious in my response for fear of being labelled a "feminist shrew." Another MPP from the New Democratic Party called on the Speaker to order the withdrawal of the remarks. I remained silent until I stepped outside the House and was faced with my first experience in the "scrum." In rugby, a scrum happens when all the players crowd around the one with the ball. In politics, the scrum consists of radio, television and newspaper reporters. They mulled around me asking what I thought of those "sexist remarks." I responded by saying I didn't think they represented the views of the majority because most people didn't cling to such ideas in this day and age.

Nonetheless, I didn't want the insult to go unanswered so I chose to deal with it in my own way. I got a copy of a cookbook called *Grits* and the next day I stood in the House on a point of privilege. "To the minister of housing [Mr. Bennett] and in absentia to the member of Fort William [Mr. Hennessy], I am happy to present personally autographed copies of a cookbook entitled *Great Grits's Recipes.* I wish to point out to the honourable members that on this enlightened side of the House our members not only let women into the legislature but also contribute in the kitchen; to wit, recipes by the member for Brant-Oxford-Norfolk [Bob Nixon], the member for Windsor-Walkerville [Bernie Newman] and the member for Niagara Falls [Vince Kerrio], among others. I am only sorry to report that there is no recipe for egg on the face. I invite the honourable members to add their own recipes to our Liberal compendium." With that, I sent over the volumes and was never assailed in the House by those two members again.

The second incident occurred when I was listening in the House to a lengthy and serious debate on the borrowing bill. As a government member droned on, a messenger arrived at my desk with a note. Curious about its contents, I opened it and found the following question: "We are running bets on how much you weigh. Please advise. B.B.R." (Boys in the Back Row).

A few months later, I was attending a parliamentary reception for an employee who was retiring from the legislature after 25 years.

At the reception, I had a chance to meet a number of new Conservative members for the first time. On this occasion, a member came up, introduced himself and handed me an envelope which had my name and seat number written on it. (Every MPP sits in an assigned seat with a corresponding seat number.) The member said, "I was going to give this to you in the House but I lost my nerve so here it is." I opened the envelope and found a colour photograph from the front page of the Toronto *Sun* showing Johnny Lombardi, the owner of CHIN Radio and the sponsor of the Toronto Bikini Beach Pageant. With Johnny were a number of bikini-clad women advertising the pageant. The member had circled the chest of one of the women and written over it "Sheila," presumably as a comment on my anatomy. I was so shocked that, for once, I followed my mother's advice, "When in doubt, keep your mouth shut." I thanked him and walked away.

Some weeks later, I was asked by the Toronto *Star* to write an article summarizing my first few months in the legislature and what it was like to be a woman in a man's world. I couldn't decide whether to write about this incident. There is an unwritten rule in every political setting, that what is said in the social circles of the House is not for public consumption. I decided, however, that I was not bound by this code, and I wrote the full story in the *Star*, omitting the name of the individual involved. My intention was not to embarrass any member but to let the public know that many stereotypes and barriers still had to be broken.

After the 1981 election, only two women were legislative newcomers, myself and Conservative Susan Fish. I was the only woman in the Liberal caucus and one of only six in the legislature. At age 28, I was an oddball in a caucus composed largely of middle-aged men with strong rural roots. My colleagues were gracious and friendly, but clearly saw me as an ornament to the party — nice to have around as long as I knew my place. One of the ironies was that most of the men in caucus thought I enjoyed the publicity that went with being the only woman. Some were even resentful when I had anything worthwhile to say. Every time I would rise in question period, one of my colleagues would mutter under his breath, "There goes Sheila. The cameras are rolling again." What he didn't realize was that I would gladly have traded my uniqueness for the chance to share some confidences and experiences with other women in caucus. Picture, if you can, the traditional caucus meeting. There we would be, 33 men and me, seated at a long, oblong table, arguing the issues of the day. Little wonder that tile drainage problems got much higher priority on our agenda than daycare or family violence. Little wonder that I felt isolated and out of place in caucus.

That feeling of loneliness haunted me throughout my work in the provincial legislature, the feeling that after a particularly heated caucus debate, you can't always share a beer with the boys. Ironically, when I was thinking of running federally, David Peterson's political assistant, Vince Borg, tried to dissuade me by suggesting that, if I moved to Ottawa, I would have to share the spotlight with other women. "There you have Monique Bégin and Judy Erola," he said. "Here, you have everything to yourself as the only woman." Little did he realize that one of the factors that drew me to the federal scene was chance to share experiences with other women politicians, people whom I had admired from afar as terrific role models. It wasn't a case of sharing the spotlight. It was a case of sharing the burden and the joy.

Examples of sexism run rampant in most businesses. Once a woman makes the decision to fight it out in a man's world, she has to be prepared to take what comes, and that includes anything from sexist comments to out-and-out passes. I was once serving on a travelling committee on child abuse. We had been hearing presentations all day and the all-party group dined together that evening. As I returned to my hotel room, I was followed by another member who invited me to his room for a drink. I refused politely, whereupon he grabbed me and started to kiss me passionately. I wanted to scream but couldn't, so I pushed him away and fled to my own room. From that day forward, my relationship with the fellow member of the legislature was strained.

How do you cope? As a newcomer, I was seen as the sweet young thing, the token woman from Hamilton Centre. It was only when the men began to realize that I would dish it out as well as take it that they began to see me in a different light. They began to understand that the boys' club atmosphere was being overtaken by the times, and that my message was being understood by the majority of Ontarians. They began to see that they were out of step with the times and a new generation of voters wanted to hear from women, from minorities, from the anti-establishment. Their only choice was to change, or to be changed — by the people in the next election.

CHAPTER

4

Into the Fire

Rule 4: To thine own self be true

What happens when personal principles and party policy collide?
One of my greatest fears in getting involved in politics was that I
would be forced at many turns to bend my principles to fit the
party line. Since I have never adapted well to regimentation, I
wondered whether I could reconcile the views of my constituents,
myself and my party.

My first test came in May 1981, when, as a provincial labour
critic, I became our party spokesperson for a controversial new
Ontario human rights code. The new code, introduced by the
governing Conservatives, included a number of positive elements
including more protection against sexual harassment and against
discrimination on the basis of handicaps or marital status. Absent
from the bill, however, was any clause to prevent discrimination
on the basis of sexual orientation. I was in a quandary. I could not
personally condone discrimination on the basis of someone's sexual
preference. After all, was it right that a person should be fired from
a job or thrown out of an apartment simply because he or she
happened to be homosexual? I could not believe that anyone who
really examined his or her conscience could condone legalized

discrimination on the basis of sexual orientation. But the political realities were quite different.

My first step, was to discuss the matter with my leader, Stuart Smith. Stuart urged me to move an amendment to include sexual orientation, even though he knew that the move would send shock waves through the conservative wing of our small Liberal caucus. "Sheila, it's something you believe in fundamentally. It's your decision, but I urge you to be courageous."

I discussed it with a number of others, whose opinions I respected, including my mother. She was horrified. "Sheila, if you have to support the amendment, that's one thing, but for heaven's sake, don't be the one moving it." I knew that if I did not move the amendment, it would be moved by the members of the New Democratic Party. Sooner or later, I would have to stand and be counted. Should I take the lead on this most important issue or leave the initiative to others?

I had to decide. I thought it over and realized I had no real choice but to stand up in the legislature and move the inclusion of a clause against discrimination on the basis of sexual orientation, because it was fundamentally wrong for any society to single out one group and deny it protection under the law.

That day, my sister was graduating from medical school. As soon as I gave my speech in the legislature, I hopped in my car and headed for the graduation ceremonies in Hamilton. When I arrived, my mother was beaming from ear to ear. I said hello and apologized for being late; I said I had spoken on the human rights issue today. In a fleeting second I saw my mother's expression change from sheer joy to confusion and fear.

"What did you say?" she asked.

I answered, "I don't believe anyone should face discrimination on the basis of sexual orientation."

Her answer: "I really wish my last name wasn't Copps."

As any mother, she feared for her daughter. A staunch Roman Catholic, she also feared a community backlash against me and our whole family. She remembered when, during my father's tenure as mayor, someone threw a rock through our window. She waited for the rocks again, but they never came.

There were no rocks, but one group flooded my riding with leaflets claiming I would force people to hire lesbian babysitters. Actually, the response on the home front was encouraging. I represented a heavily ethnic, working-class riding and expected some opposition. But when I explained I was only fighting for everyone's right to equality, they understood.

I only wish the legislature had been so understanding. I spent the next months meeting with interested groups and attempting to convince my Liberal party colleagues to support me on the issue. Since the leader had stated that there would be a free vote on this matter as an issue of conscience, I had to fight not only the government but those in our caucus who opposed the notion of equal rights for homosexuals. I set up meetings, I analyzed and educated, I helped organize lobbies and letter-writing campaigns, all gearing up to the presentation of the bill in the House. A number of gay groups had come into the chamber for the vote and, as the roll call was taken, they chained themselves to the walls and chanted and shouted. The then minister of agriculture pointed his finger at me and roared "These are your friends. You're disgusting." When women fought for their rights, they were forced into chains to be heard, and so it was for gay groups.

The gays and I lost that time. But in losing, I learned an invaluable lesson: I must follow my own conscience in politics. If I do what I believe to be right, public support may follow. But if I wake up tomorrow out of office, I must be able to live with the decisions I have made and the issues I have pursued.

The issue also taught me that even when my closest friends or family disagree, I must follow my own conscience. The strength of the family is that disagreements need not break those family bonds. Indeed, the sense that 'we're in this together' grows even stronger in the face of adversity.

I never dreamed that my first major battle would be on gay rights. But in retrospect, human rights and equality are liberal issues which any Canadian can support.

5

The Flora Syndrome

Rule 5: Never say never

I had been in the legislature only six months when Liberal leader Stuart Smith announced his intention to resign. With only 34 Liberal seats in a 125-member legislature, Stuart felt after two elections that enough was enough. An innovator and a thinker, the former psychiatrist found his role in opposition particularly taxing because it meant he could never move ahead with his ideas. His job was to criticize, not to construct, so he stepped down and opened the way for a leadership race.

The convention was set for the following February but already the candidates had begun to emerge. The front runner was David Peterson, the affable MPP from London Centre who had come a mere 45 votes behind Stuart in the leadership race of 1976. David was ready, indeed eager for a second chance. James Breithaupt, longstanding member and justice critic for the Liberal party, was seriously interested. A third contestant was John Sweeney, a former educator whose experience with his own ten children had given him a particular mission in politics. And then there was Richard Thomas, affectionately known as 'Ben' from his role in television commercials, where the robust woodsman endorsed a particular brand of bacon. Richard's passion was the environment, and he saw the Liberal party as a vehicle to force the province to come to grips with the growing problem of pollution.

Needless to say, the inside track was with David Peterson. David had quietly been organizing throughout the province. His family credentials were impeccable; his brother was a member of Parliament and his sister-in-law worked for Pierre Trudeau. His father was a signatory to the CCF Regina manifesto and his father-in-law was former chairman of the PC Canada Fund. He looked unbeatable. David's family and the family of his wife, the former Shelley Matthews, had lived and breathed politics most of their lives. David had studied law and then run a successful family electronics business. He became a provincial member in 1975. He had all the makings of a successful politician. David was so clearly in the lead that the leadership race had all the makings of a coronation.

But if the Liberals were going to have the kind of leadership convention which would lead to party renewal and a chance to topple the Tories for the first time in more than 40 years, we had to add some element of challenge to the race for the leadership. We couldn't afford a shoo-in. I searched the caucus for potential candidates. I spoke to Sean Conway, urging him to throw his hat into the ring. I challenged others, including a couple of federal cabinet ministers, to consider seeking the leadership. Everywhere I went, no response.

Meanwhile, I began to feel some pressure to run myself. Again, my first reaction was one of horror. No one in their right mind would vote for me. I was 28, had been in the legislature less than one year and had no business challenging the party establishment in a race. But I also recognized that a lacklustre convention would send a message that no one really cared who won the Liberal leadership.

Perhaps my Irish got up again — my Irish is always pretty active. Perhaps the gambler in me just couldn't say no. Two days after my

29th birthday, I entered the race for the leadership of Her Majesty's Loyal Opposition in the most populated province in Canada.

My decision wasn't as impulsive as it might seem. Before I agreed, I made sure of two things: I wouldn't be humiliated at the polls and I wouldn't go into personal debt.

I made sure of the first by canvassing a number of key Liberals before I made up my mind. What did they think? Did they have any suggestions? Ideas? Concerns? The second, I determined by securing a financial chairman who I could trust to deliver the goods. My choice, on federal cabinet minister Bob Kaplan's recommendation, was Monte Kwinter, chairman of the Toronto Harbour Commission. I met with Monte and proposed my plan to run for the leadership if he could guarantee a base budget of $30,000. So much he promised and so much he raised. In fact, we ran the cheapest campaign of any candidate. My campaign manager, Joe Cruden, was another political veteran who knew that you don't necessarily win elections or leaderships with dollars.

We turned frugality into a virtue. I couldn't afford to travel by plane but, as a member of the legislature, I automatically received a train pass on the Ontario Northland. Following Diefenbaker's lead, I took to the rails. I wanted to meet people in their own communities. And how better to do it than by train? On New Year's Eve, 1981, I spent seventeen hours on the train between Sudbury and Thunder Bay. The bar car ran out of beer at 9 pm but my sister Mary and brother-in-law Barry Sutherland managed to bootleg a bottle of champagne which we cracked at midnight, somewhere between White River and Thunder Bay. We stayed with friends and relatives rather than at hotels, ostensibly because we wanted to get back to the people but really because we couldn't afford expensive accommodation. The Liberal party had organized a tour through the north by plane and through southwestern Ontario by bus. We opted for the northern plane trip at a cost of some $650 each, but we declined the bus tour.

One newspaper reported that I stayed off the bus tour because

I couldn't take the rough and tumble of the boys on the bus. Little did the journalists know that while my colleagues were being bused at a cost of $225 per person and bedded at major hotels en route, we toured the same events on a shoestring. Before I decided to pass up the bus tour, a fellow candidate warned me that I was making a big mistake, because I wouldn't be seen as part of the team. In fact, my reasons were purely financial. In the end my total campaign bill was about half the average and one-quarter that of the ultimate winner and future premier, David Peterson.

The decision to stay off the campaign bus also gave me the freedom to arrive at meetings before any other candidates and chat with delegates long after the bus pulled away for the night. Ours was a real grass-roots campaign. I slept in the homes of supporters on the campaign trail and did everything possible to meet the maximum number of people without spending money. It's a good thing I had plenty of energy because our campaign pace was hectic. You probably think of a leadership campaign as a bit glamorous, flooded with the glare of the television cameras. What you don't see are the hundreds of lonely hours spent on the road simply getting from one meeting to another.

I remember one particularly frustrating morning when I rose at 5 am after four hours sleep to drive from London to St. Catharines, a distance of about 140 kilometres, for an 8:30 am radio show. It was still dark outside when I left my sister's house. The wind was howling and the snow was blowing along a lonely stretch of Route 401, when the tire on my car blew out. I had no flashlight and couldn't free the jack because it was screwed down so tight. Every time a truck went by, its slipstream threw me against the car amid a swirl of blinding snow. Practically in tears and swearing to myself, I kept asking whether politics was really worth this kind of hassle. Suddenly, a transport trucker for a beer company stopped and offered to help. Within minutes I was back in my car and made it to my radio interview only a few minutes late.

The reaction to my campaign was (to put it mildly) interesting.

Wherever we went, the crowds were warm and supportive. After more than 40 years in the wilderness, Liberals in Ontario seemed to be willing to throw off the stereotypes and consider someone absolutely unorthodox, a woman. But I found the press and the party establishment were nowhere near as liberated as the average voting delegate.

The press immediately wrote me off as an absolute long shot. They focused their attention on the front runner, David Peterson, and on two longtime members from the Kitchener area, Jim Breithaupt and John Sweeney. Reporters kept asking me, "What about the Flora syndrome?" The press remembered, and remembered well, the predicament facing Flora MacDonald when she sought the leadership of the Progressive Conservative party in 1976. She was encouraged, cajoled and supported before the convention, but in the crunch, her support failed to translate into votes. The press decided that Flora's experience was typical of any woman's attempt to seek the leadership of her party.

We used every possible means to get our message out, as long as it met one condition: don't spend any money. Sometimes that meant turning disadvantage into advantage.

The day the candidates were to embark on the tour through Northern Ontario we were all scheduled to arrive at the airstrip in the early afternoon. Below-zero weather created flying problems and we were told the plane would be delayed a couple of hours before takeoff. While the other candidates were sharing coffee and warming up in the hangar, I slipped away to telephone the radio stations in Thunder Bay, explaining why we wouldn't be arriving at the all-candidates meeting on time. My message was broadcast live while everyone was still waiting for the plane to take off.

38

I had some news sense, but I needed a lot of work in other areas. One of the lessons you learn early on in politics is that you are public property and you'd better get used to public criticism. That criticism has to do not only with what you say, but how you say it, and even what you wear while you're saying it.

I'll never forget the time that the campaign committee called a meeting to tell me I dressed like a frump and I should change my whole wardrobe before the big day. Here I was sitting in a room surrounded by people (mostly men) who wanted to tell me how to dress. My first reaction was to blow up: "I am what I am, and people will have to take me that way."

When I had a chance to cool down I agreed to visit a shop in Toronto, appropriately called the Working Woman, with E-day chairman, Malka Rosenberg, so that we could pick out an outfit for the leadership weekend. The committee was right. As a woman, the way I dressed was written about and commented on in a way that would never plague a male candidate. During the northern tour, one journalist wrote that my hairstyle could best be described as the Roman-helmet look and that I had worn the same outfit twice. No one ever commented on the timeworn blue pinstripe suits favoured by my competitors — or on their bald spots.

My campaign team was incredible. While I was stumping the province, they were planning a strategy which would catapult me into contention. Although we were broke, we had access to a computer from midnight until 6 am. One of the organizers, Michael Lebovic, was in the business of professional telephone sales. He developed a telephone script which we used to interview each delegate. We had identified a group of leaners, delegates who hadn't already made up their minds. We called and interviewed them in depth, sticking strictly to our script. This allowed us to garner certain information: What were the delegates'concerns? Why were they going to the convention? What issues interested them? As soon as the phone call was complete, we sent a personalized computer letter to the delegate from me outlining their concerns and what I intended to do about them. This was the only piece of correspondence we sent to the delegates in advance of the convention. While other candidates with bigger budgets were flooding the postal service, our personalized computer letter hit home.

Every committee decision was reached by consensus. Although this sometimes meant hours of haggling at Saturday morning meetings, the end result was that everyone felt involved in the process. We even went so far as to make our own signs. We also agreed that the only giveaways the weekend of the convention would be our policy booklets and signs. No hats, no hoopla. Ours was to be the 'serious' campaign. Our strategy paid off. In fact, our delegate tracking showed that I was right up there behind David.

In the last week before the convention, the political activity in our camp reached a crescendo. I received endorsements from the Toronto *Star* and *The Globe and Mail*.

But as the date drew near, it became clear that I would be fighting not only the stereotyped view of women, but the party establishment. During the final weeks of the leadership, the movers, shakers and rainmakers of the national party started to make their moves in the provincial scene. The backroom boys in Ottawa, coupled with the Liberal caucus in Toronto were sending out a clear and unanimous message. They were solidly behind David Peterson. However, I had the support of seven federal cabinet ministers. In the last week, we convinced six of them to sign their names to a joint press release endorsing me. They were an impressive group: Bob Kaplan, Jim Fleming, Judy Erola, Charles Caccia, John Munro and Jean-Jacques Blais. We were saving the seventh, Eugene Whelan, for the weekend, as our surprise nominator.

I was heartened when, during a visit to Ottawa to meet with the Liberal caucus, I literally bumped into Prime Minister Trudeau while he made his way to question period. The prime minister asked what I was doing in Ottawa, and I replied that I was running for the provincial leadership and was out on the hustings. He suggested a meeting at a later date.

Everything seemed to be falling into place. With the boost from newspaper endorsements and the prime minister's personal interest, I felt I was on a roll. But instead of contenting myself with a mere social call, I naively assumed that I could discuss business with Mr. Trudeau. I was ushered into his office, spent a few moments admiring the incredible Inuit art which softened the rather ascetic interior, and then launched into my checklist.

"Could the prime minister please ask his friend, Keith Davey, to lay off the heavy-handed selling job of David Peterson?" Because David's sister-in-law worked in the prime minister's office, I felt that it was critical that there be absolutely no hint of PMO involvement and that Mr. Davey's "persuasive" approach was carrying things a little too far.

I also asked the prime minister whether he could give Eugene Whelan special permission to leave the House of Commons early on the night of the nominations. Eugene had offered to nominate me, and his support among the southwestern farmers could have been a perfect foil for my urban roots. Unfortunately, the federal Tories, in their continuing attempts to make life miserable for the

Liberals, had ordered a Friday night vote to delay the federal members' arrival at the convention.

I chatted with Mr. Trudeau for 40 minutes. He said he had no control over the doings of Keith Davey and could not allow Eugene to leave early. He thought it would be much simpler to simply postpone the convention. Throughout our conversation, Trudeau smiled that enigmatic smile and asked me, with utter innocence, why someone like me was interested in pursuing a role in politics. I was interested in discussing the campaign process with him but Trudeau kept staring at me with those riveting Gallic eyes and telling me what a beautiful smile I had. I persisted. I desperately wanted to get Eugene to the nomination meeting on time. Trudeau did not want to be bothered with such minor logistical details. He couldn't understand why the whole convention could not be postponed for one hour to permit the arrival of the federal Liberals from Ottawa. He didn't seem to realize that even in Liberal circles, the provincial party didn't want to look like the junior partner to 'The Feds', particularly during a leadership race.

Trudeau's naiveté about the internal bickering that affects all political parties was almost charming. Here was a man who had led our party for fourteen years without recognizing the acute rivalry between the federal Liberals and provincial organizations that were struggling to maintain their own identities. It wasn't that he didn't care. He simply didn't understand that it might present a problem to postpone a provincial leadership convention.

I left the meeting absolutely empty-handed but totally smitten; the leader of our country had taken 40 minutes from his busy day to discuss my leadership plans. I had succumbed — as almost everyone who met him did — to the sphinx's inscrutable charm. Needless to say, Keith Davey kept working and Eugene did not arrive in Toronto in time to nominate me.

Just as I could not convince the prime minister, so I could not sway the Liberal establishment, which seemed to believe that Ontario was not ready for a woman, and a 29-year-old woman at that. My main opposition came from the MUPPIES (male urban professionals) who saw the involvement of more women as a threat to the traditional hold they had on the party system.

Contrary to popular myth, I had tremendous support from women — young, middle-aged and elderly. Many elderly women told me that they wished that they'd had the same chances when they were young. Young men and women, who saw themselves as underdogs in the political power structure, identified with me and the brand of liberalism I espoused.

The convention weekend arrived. Friday night was devoted to a tribute to Stuart Smith, who had given the party hope when we were being written off. My group had decided to play a low-key role and refrain from partisan cheering during the opening ceremonies; all our efforts were concentrated on Saturday.

The first crisis erupted Friday night when it became clear that Eugene Whelan would arrive in time for the nomination, despite our best efforts to whisk him to the Sheraton Centre in Toronto as soon as he disembarked from the plane. With a half-hour to go, we needed a backup nominator. We had tried to convince an MPP to speak, but to no avail. At the last moment, northern delegate and campaign organizer, John Lentowicz, a past provincial candidate, was called up to write and deliver the opening nomination. Pitted against the MPPs who were nominating other candidates, John set the tone for the convention — the establishment versus the little people.

The rest of the night was spent in hotel rooms meeting with

small groups of undecided delegates from across the province. All eyes were focused on the main event, the Saturday speeches. My speech would be critical to my success. People were expecting fire and brimstone from me while they believed David's forté would be organization, not oratory.

Those in the know said that David would have been elected leader against Stuart Smith in 1976 but for a disastrous performance during the speeches. He wasn't about to make the same mistake again. Throughout the week his advisors publicly mused about a possible 'disaster'; if he just survived the speech, they would be happy. In fact, he did more than survive; he delivered what some described as the best political speech of his career. It wasn't a barnburner but it certainly showed that he could deliver the goods under very difficult circumstances.

As for me, I succumbed to 'leaderitis'. Throughout the campaign I had been criticized for speaking from my heart, not my head. The press suggested I was too emotional. This time, I opted for the head, with a measured speaking style to prove that I had 'the right stuff'; that I could speak like a premier. My campaign committee had already battled it out on the speech. Some wanted me to maintain my direct style, others thought I should take a more low-key approach. In the end, the voice factor was the major reason for my change. As a woman, whenever I belt it out my voice tends to rise an octave or so. In the heat of the moment, the committee felt that that octave would distract from the content of my speech. In retrospect, it meant I was reined in and more subdued than my supporters had expected. If I had stuck to my own style my supporters could have raised the roof.

I knew I hadn't done as well as I wanted, but I felt warmed by the wave of enthusiasm sweeping the crowd. What I lacked in my speech, my supporters made up for in enthusiasm. They shrieked, they screamed, they waved their signs. A sea of black and yellow Sheila signs swept across the campaign floor. Our colours (chosen to reflect those of the Hamilton Tiger Cats' football team) were highly visible against the reds and blacks of David Peterson and the designer hues of some other candidates. My campaign workers were young, tireless, strong-lunged and utterly shameless. They stood on chairs and cheered until they were hoarse, in contrast to the restrained floor demonstration of the well-suited Peterson supporters.

One newspaper reporter described our supporters as moonies, mindless in their devotion to a cause. From the opening hour of the convention, when volunteers from each campaign charged onto the convention floor to set up signs, it was clear the Copps team was travelling on a high. Friend and political organizer Don Drury, towering well over six feet, had organized our team to make sure that Copps signs were plastered all over the convention hall. What we lacked in manufactured goodies (the other candidates flooded the convention floor with free food, flowers and even jogging jackets) we made up for in sheer enthusiasm. As we left the convention floor after the speeches, our workers circled around the escalators on four floors of the Sheraton Centre and shouted my name. We thought we could feel the wind of change.

The candidates danced the night away at various campaign parties, while the workers hit the floor, buttonholing each delegate in search of support. That's where the fight turned nasty.

Anonymous notes circulated, accusing me of lesbian tendencies. One MPP suggested that I wasn't psychologically strong enough to handle the pressure of leadership. Several senior caucus members suggested privately that they would resign if I were chosen leader. Saturday night was the beginning of the ABS (Anyone But Sheila) move, where Liberal forces decided that they were going to stop my efforts at all costs.

The Peterson people sensed the momentum building in the Copps camp. It seemed that every gathering on the Saturday night campaign circuit was full of Copps supporters, vigorously lobbying to bring the undecided onside. Peterson people were tracking delegates hourly and pushed the panic button in the small hours of the morning. At 3 am, all MPPs supporting David were called to an emergency meeting to assess the damage. They were still publicly predicting a first-ballot victory, but privately they expressed real concern about the momentum in our organization. A letter began circulating, signed by several caucus members who threatened to resign their seats if I were elected. Copps supporters were button-holed in hotel corridors and asked if they knew about my psychological problems. Snide innuendoes about my sexual preferences actually prompted a couple of fist fights.

I missed all the excitement. As the candidate, it was my job to meet as many delegates as possible and to leave the lobbying to others. That meant sticking to a tight schedule where every minute of the evening was accounted for. We even commandeered a freight elevator at the Sheraton Centre so we wouldn't waste any time getting from one hotel room to another to meet with undecided voters. It was one supporter's responsibility simply to hang on to the elevator all night. We communicated by walkie-talkie. After the meetings, we travelled to every convention party. The highlight for our team was the jazz group from my hometown singing "Sheila, Sheila" to the tune of "New York, New York." The whole room was rocking. No high-priced Toronto band could compete with the level of excitement in our camp and the dance floor was packed.

Later that night, I sneaked away with a friend for a quick bite at Barberian's, a late-night Toronto spot known for good food. Who should I bump into but CBC's Mike Duffy. Mike sent a couple of Irish coffees over to our table with his compliments. He also leaked some top-secret CBC information: a CBC poll had shown that David and I were running neck and neck. I didn't know whether to scream or smile. I had only in my wildest dreams entertained the faintest hope that I might win. Now, less than twelve hours before the vote, it seemed that I just might pull off a victory, and I was scared stiff. I finally hit the sack at 2 am, but woke up in a cold sweat wondering what would happen; not if I lost, but if I won. I was frightened. I knew the difficulties, not only of winning the convention, but also of convincing the caucus of mostly older men that I could work with them and be a credit to our party.

On Sunday morning at about 8:30, I made my way down to the voting hall. As I descended the escalator, I encountered a phalanx of Peterson supporters. The entire Liberal caucus had risen early to make sure they impressed upon all the delegates the need to support their chosen candidate. The leaflet said it all. More than 80 per cent of the caucus supported David Peterson. What the leaflet failed to state, caucus members made explicit; a couple of them went on television to say they would resign if I were elected. I made my way past them and into the hall for the only thing that counted: the vote.

The count was long. We sang and chatted, and I politicked in the meantime. We knew that the first ballot would be decisive. David needed 1,000 to take him over the top. Anything under 900 would give the second candidate a real shot at it. I was frightened of showing what I felt, forcing myself to look calmer and more cheerful than I was. I was damned if I'd succumb to the myth that a woman can't stand the strain.

The numbers came in: Peterson, 966; Copps, 636; Thomas, 234; Breithaupt, 130; and Sweeney, 122. I knew I had no real chance, but I had to hang on for my supporters. The press was poised. Their assessment was predictable. One reporter leaned over and stated point blank, "An obviously shaken Sheila Copps is facing the results." I responded, "I am not shaken." I was, in fact, comforting my campaign manager, Joe Cruden, who had put his heart and soul into the effort.

At the same time, according to plan, I immediately hit the hustings, urging my supporters to stick with me through a second ballot, hoping to draw new support. We had to smash the Flora syndrome. Even if we could not win on the second ballot, it was critical that our numbers grow. Otherwise, my candidacy would be written off as a fluke — another woman getting token first ballot support.

Supporters moved out into the hall. On the first night of the convention, each of my people had been assigned a 'buddy' in the other camps. It was now their job to convince their buddies to come over to our side. Obviously, the Peterson supporters were unshakeable. We were aiming at those in other camps who would be looking for somewhere else to go.

John Sweeney and Jim Breithaupt both dropped off the ballot. Breithaupt immediately swung over to Peterson, but John Sweeney turned his delegates loose. Our people were begging Richard Thomas to drop out, but he insisted that he was in until the last ballot. He was finally convinced to drop out, but it was too late to get his name off the second ballot.

The final showdown would prove whether our campaign had depth or whether it was another case of the Flora syndrome. In my heart, I knew the writing was on the wall. But I had to keep my chin up to show that women don't break down at the least disappointment. In fact, another candidate, John Sweeney, was moved to tears, but since he was a man, that seemed an under-standable response to an incredibly charged moment. Emotions in the jammed convention room were running high. Many people were in tears. Even a reporter who had followed me throughout the campaign was crying as she gave in to the emotional crush of the moment we had all been waiting for. But I couldn't afford to weep because that would mark me — and other women — as a cry baby, unable to take the strain. I kept my chin up, kept cam-paigning, even though I knew the next ballot would end it.

The results vindicated us: Peterson, 1,136; Copps, 774; Thomas, 148. In the face of certain defeat our support had grown by 138 votes. We had shown that it was possible for a woman to be a credible leadership candidate. I immediately bolted through the mêlée of reporters and delegates to join David on the stage and move that the decision to make him our leader be a unanimous one.

Although the loss was a disappointment, I knew in my heart it was for the best. I joined my party in saluting our new leader and I began the job of rebuilding broken bridges in my own Liberal caucus.

CHAPTER

6

The Politics of Power

Rule 6: Never look back

On Monday morning I was back at my desk, beginning the job of regaining my place in the Liberal caucus. Funny — when I had been the 'sweet young thing' from Hamilton Centre, the only woman in caucus, I'd been no great threat. But the leadership convention changed that. For the first time, the men in my caucus realized that women could be more than tokens in our party, that we could wield influence — even power. That notion frightened a number of my colleagues, who had heretofore only dealt with competition from men. While I had failed in my bid to lead our party, I had shown that it might be possible for another woman at another time. That realization threatened men who might themselves seek greater political roles.

We politicians are an egotistical lot. While we are motivated by the greater public good, there is no denying that we love the recognition that comes from public office. Politics may never make you rich or powerful, but it does give your ego a chance to expand. For that reason, politicians are a powerfully competitive group. We have our principles and beliefs, but male or female, we love and crave the emotional boost, and we compete among our peers for our share of the public spotlight. As the only woman in caucus, I had reached a delicate balance with my colleagues. That balance was shattered on that convention weekend.

It became increasingly clear to me that, while my bid for the leadership had strengthened my stock in the party, it had put me on the outside of the caucus looking in. I had to do everything I could to regain the confidence of my peers, to show them that I was not there to rock the boat. Having seen me once as a possible threat, they had difficulty in believing that I was there to help our leader not to thwart him. David was super. He immediately called me to ask how he could involve me on the team. The Liberal leadership race had emphasized certain concerns about Ontario's future. One of those concerns was the need for a new approach to health care.

David asked me to take on a new responsibility, that of health critic. He also asked me to head up a task force which would travel Ontario to examine the fundamental problems facing our health system. I immediately plunged into the job. The task force team visited a dozen communities across Ontario and spoke with several hundred groups and individuals. The result was a document entitled *Health Care in Ontario: On The Critical List*, which chronicled some of the fundamental problems facing our system and proposed some remedies.

We talked not only to doctors but to others involved in health care — nurses, orderlies and allied services — to find out how the direction of health care could be changed. It became increasingly clear that health care, like politics, is a power game, involving a constant struggle to break away from traditional solutions.

The committee included myself and MPPs Bill Wrye, Ron Van Horne and Hugh O'Neil. After an exhaustive series of public hearings across Ontario, we came to a clearer understanding of the power struggle involved in medicine. How can you control costs when you have a system that is based on quantity, not quality, of service? The more patients a doctor sees, the more money he or she makes.

Our recommendation to the Liberal caucus was that the report include a series of changes to health care in Ontario. We asked for an end to OHIP premiums and an increase in funding for non-traditional health service organizations.

One of our major recommendations involved a proposed ban on extra billing. As a committee, we believed that extra billing must be stopped, not only because it was eroding the guarantee of universal access but because it symbolized service based on dollars rather than quality care. For years, the position of the Liberal party had been the same as the Conservatives. We supported extra billing while the New Democratic Party opposed it. Given that levels of opting out had risen to 15 per cent overall and to 50 and 60 per cent in certain specialties, our committee believed that this would be the perfect time for the Liberal party to change its policy.

We argued our case very strongly in caucus, but we were overruled. A number of caucus members, including the leader, did not want to approve any change in policy on extra billing. They wanted to avoid a confrontation with the medical profession and felt that the present situation was acceptable. As health critic, I was frustrated by a system that seemed more interested in entrenching power bases and maintaining the status quo than in encouraging the evolution of real health care — an evolution espoused in Marc Lalonde's ten-year-old report on new health perspectives. Our caucus seemed unprepared to challenge the traditional medical establishment for fear of a backlash.

I believed the people were ready for a change in Ontario public policy on extra billing. Obviously under David Peterson's leadership, the Liberals in Ontario have accomplished just that. It is not by supporting established power structures that the Liberal party has ever achieved positive social change. It is only by challenging the status quo, by venturing into dangerous political waters, that our party has succeeded in capturing the imagination of the public.

In covering new territory, the health system is certainly the place to start. As a province, Ontario had lost touch with the reality of health care delivery. The medical model claimed that all problems could be solved by increasing the availability of hospital beds, or augmenting the costly technology which was already pricing us out of the marketplace. We were so mired in this system that we forgot the changing demographics of our province and country. We cannot always find a cure. The hospital-based approach to health care does nothing for the increasing numbers of elderly who are forced into substandard nursing homes or denied good health care at home because our system is based on institutionalization.

Women bring a perspective both to medicine and to politics which allows them to break away from the stereotypes. Let's take a look at pregnancy and childbirth. Having a baby is a most natural thing! For a healthy woman, with adequate nutrition and good prenatal care, the birth itself should be eventful but intervention-free. And yet in the last ten years, Canada has become the second-most caesareaned country in the world after the United States. We have an increasingly specialized medical profession which is trained in early detection and intervention, which treats childbirth as an illness rather than a natural phenomenon, and which increasingly hordes authority and responsibility for even the most natural and easy birth.

We women understand that childbirth is a natural phenomenon, not a 'women's illness'. But what we do not realize is that politics can make a difference in how we live our lives — even in health care. As I worked in the area, I became convinced that the only way to break down barriers, the only way to encourage a return to the notion of health care rather than illness care, was to begin to break down some of the power structures. But that's more easily said than done.

Nurses are engaged in a struggle to take more responsibility for

53

primary health care. The only area in Ontario in which nurses have an opportunity to fulfil their potential as health practitioners is north of the 60th parallel where doctors are rare. Similarly, midwives worked in a kind of legal limbo; their profession had never been licensed until a recent change by the new Liberal government in Ontario.

As the Opposition health critic, I sat (as the only woman) on a committee which reexamined the Public Health Act for the first time in more than 100 years. When the act was first passed, it was meant to cover a variety of problems — sanitation, epidemiology, and so forth. Obviously these are still important, but the emphasis of public health had changed enormously since the act was passed.

As a committee, we were struck by some startling data on the incidence of teenaged mothers. More and more children are having and keeping their children. Some 90 per cent of teenage mothers were keeping their children compared to just 50 per cent only a few years before.

A university research team faced the committee with some compelling suggestions for reducing the number of teenage pregnancies. They presented data which showed that, in communities where teenagers had access to birth control information and family planning, there was a significant drop in adolescent pregnancies. In neighbouring communities where access to information was limited, there was a corresponding increase in teenage pregnancies. Their recommendations supported by nursing groups, teachers and others, proposed that the provincial government give all public health departments a mandate for primary prevention of adolescent pregnancy. The emphasis was to be education — contraception not abortion.

We heard overwhelming evidence on why it was important to address this problem. Unless we did something to reduce the incidence of teenaged pregnancy, we would be helping to create a social time bomb. Contrary to popular myth, the evidence showed that many young women knew little about family planning. Some were simply ignorant of the facts of life. Yet in many communities, there was absolutely nowhere they could turn to for help or guidance. The committee rejected the argument that sex education would encourage promiscuity. Instead we agreed that many young people were already sexually active and it was foolish to ignore the fact or to deny them help. The consequences were far too serious.

Throughout the hearings we agreed that the number one public health issue among young people was adolescent pregnancy. We saw examples of the risks of becoming a too-young parent. A fifteen-year-old single mother who quits school and lives on public assistance is usually lonely and frightened. She hasn't fully outgrown her own childhood and is not ready to accept responsibility for another human being. Incidences of child abuse, malnutrition and cyclical welfare dependence are high. The committee agreed that one way of breaking the cycle was to educate young people about the consequences of active sexuality and the possible methods of preventing conception.

But when the time came for a vote, the committee gave in to the pleas of the minister of health, who argued that we could not saddle every public health unit in the province with the responsibility of preventing adolescent pregnancy. Why not? The minister said that he was not prepared to impose his morality or the morality of the committee on any community in our province. In short, he wanted to play it safe politically. By doing so, he helped to condemn a whole generation of young women — some to helpless dependency, even more to the difficulties of single parenting.

When the government refused to support any change, I moved an amendment which would have forced public health units to provide contraception information in every community. The amendment was killed by the Conservative majority in committee.

I tell this story to show how the predominantly-male Conservative elite maintains the status quo (and the status quo excludes women). If the Conservative membership on the committee had included women, the vote might have been quite different. It's easy for a man, who could never be pregnant, to deny others any access to information on contraception. That vote would be much more difficult for a woman, who can understand in a direct way the issues about which men can only hypothesize.

Not every woman in politics is going to follow the same blueprint for social change. But her understanding of issues is fundamentally different from a man's, and she can bring a unique insight either to government or to opposition.

I am not ashamed of saying I am a feminist, that I fight for women. I make no apologies, just as a farmer would never dream of apologizing for fighting for farmers, nor would a businessman apologize for promoting the interests of his group. Women make up an absolute majority in this country. Why should our interests be considered trivial? Why should we leave it to others to represent us, and to fight our battles? Who should make decisions on health care during pregnancy or on contraception? A man, no matter how good a father he may be, can't carry and bear children. It's up to us, the women of Canada, to look out for ourselves and our own.

We are the majority, but we leave it up to others to represent our interests and fight our battles. Who better to represent the majority of Canadians than women? And who better to make decisions about issues like adolescent pregnancy than that segment of the population that understands pregnancy best? — the women of Canada.

7

The 64 Cent Solution

Rule 7: United we stand (sometimes)

David Peterson's commitment to improve the lot of women in the Liberal party was genuine. He set up a special committee to encourage good candidates and to reach out to women not yet involved in the political process. The women's perspectives committee organized the first fundraising drive to assist women candidates, highlighted by the annual Margaret Campbell dinner. The committee also worked to recruit good women candidates. David meant to bring more women into the mainstream. He was also prepared to give issues affecting women a major place in his election platform. One of those issues was equal pay for work of equal value.

In the political process, we have a device known as the private member's bill. Most of these bills end up going nowhere, because they are not part of the government's political agenda. However, if your timing is right, a private member's bill can be important. I introduced one such bill; a resolution calling upon the government to give legal force to the principle of equal pay for work of equal value. I deliberately kept the resolution simple so the government could not find a reason to vote against it.

Meanwhile, the Equal Pay Coalition, comprised of women in

the public and private sectors, had just launched a major campaign for changes in the law. The pressure was on the government to do something to bridge the wage gap between men and women. The Ministry of Labour had issued a report, and events conspired to bring greater public attention to the problem.

When the time finally arrived for my bill to be heard in the House, it became the focus of a major legislative debate. Members of all three parties spoke in favour of the bill, pointing out the tremendous wage disparities between men and women and and the need to move toward economic equality. When the bill came to a vote, we witnessed an unprecedented sight: every Conservative in the House rose to support it. That was probably my proudest day in the provincial legislature. All three parties had agreed on the need for new laws to provide a climate where women could compete equally in the marketplace. Gone were the days when a government switchboard operator with a grade twelve education and years of experience would earn $4,000 less than a parking lot attendant whose only qualification was the ability to speak English. Gone were the days when the university librarian earned substantially less than the university gardener.

Or so I thought. Political reality being what it is, it was necessary for the government to support the private member's bill because it could not oppose a principle which had so much public support. But the Conservatives really had no intention of implementing the principle. We waited for some action on the resolution. And we waited and we waited. The government's response, instead of the promised legislation, was a task force which took all of one week to discuss the question.

One of the government's key witnesses at the hearings was an American economist, brought up at public expense, to describe how the American equivalent of equal value legislation had been a disaster. It became clear during his testimony that he also opposed the minimum wage because it interfered with the marketplace. He may also have believed in the tooth fairy; the question never arose.

58

The hearing ended and absolutely nothing was done even to consider implementation of equal value legislation. The same government that had unanimously supported my motion marched out all the time-worn arguments: it's impossible to compare two different jobs in the same company, valuing work is too subjective, and so forth. My response? Of course, all salary scales are subjective but when you sit down and quantify skill, effort, working conditions and experience, you at least take the gender out of salary levels. But the government went on dilly-dallying, and women in Ontario continued to earn 64 cents for every dollar earned by a man.

The government used much the same tactics to deal with — or rather not to deal with — the question of family violence. It had no objection to study teams, task forces and investigatory groups, as long as it didn't have to do anything. The Tories found themselves regretfully unable to supply funds to improve access to transition houses or to upgrade services for abused children. Lip service seemed to be the Conservatives' strongest point.

The Conservatives' failure to support universal daycare meant that many children were receiving care of questionable quality and thousands of 'latchkey' kids had no care at all. Think of a secretary with three small children: she makes maybe $14,000 per year, and has to pay at least $200 per week for child care, unless she can find subsidized facilites. The Tories behaved as though we still lived in the 1950s, ignoring the increase in single-parent and two-career families.

We often hear our politicians say that our greatest natural resource is our children. Yet when it comes to balancing the budget, our children always seem to occupy the lowest rung on the ladder.

What politicians do understand is the ballot box. Even though the Conservatives did nothing but study the equal-value resolution during their term in office, when the provincial election was called in 1984 they promised new laws. The promises were part of a last-ditch effort to woo new voters into their fold; voters who had seen the revitalized Liberal party under David Peterson contrasted to the tired old Conservative party of the 1950s, now headed by Frank Miller.

While a central campaign plank for the Liberals was equal-pay legislation, the Tories failed to address the issue until a few days before the election. Even that move wasn't enough to turn the tide of public opinion. The voters spoke loudly, and for the first time in 43 years more people voted for the Liberals. A new progressive team, supporting positive legislation on health care, women's rights and minority rights was swept into power after the Conservatives lost a non-confidence vote on the speech from the throne. And although I had worked almost eight years to see it happen, I would not be there to take that walk across the floor to the first Ontario Liberal government in my lifetime.

8

From the Frying Pan

Rule 8: Never fear the fire

In 1984, after more than three years in opposition and almost eight in full-time politics, I began to feel the opposition itch. Would I ever get the chance to test my theories about improving our society through legislative change? I knew in my heart it was much easier to govern from the opposition benches and I wondered if I could live up to the challenge of government.

Bill Davis, the amiable, popular Conservative premier was well-entrenched, and even the most optimistic Liberals wondered privately if he could ever be beaten. I enjoyed my work on the hustings but the frustration of the opposition process was beginning to take its toll. I had not considered leaving Queen's Park, but events transpired which seemed to leave me no choice.

The federal Liberal party called an election, and the member of Parliament for Hamilton East stepped down. John Munro decided to call it quits after more than a quarter-century of public service. Many of us urged him not to resign. We thought he was too much of a political animal to enjoy life without politics. But he was determined to go, disheartened by his failed bid for the Liberal leadership and the subsequent loss of a cabinet post.

Once his decision was made, we had little time to find a new candidate; the writ was about to be issued. In some respects, I felt a sense of *dèja vu*. I didn't want to leave the provincial legislature, particularly since I was the only woman in the Liberal caucus and we were making definite strides in our political work. But I thought I should follow my own advice to other women: If opportunity comes your way, take it, even if the timing isn't right. You may never get the chance again.

I feared two things. First, I thought we might lose the federal seat; and second, I didn't want to succumb to the opposition mentality, which afflicts parties after too many years of challenging government without the responsibility of running a province or a country.

My family and friends were split on whether I should resign my provincial seat. My sister, Mary, a member of the provincial Liberal executive, was on the phone hourly from her home in London, urging me not to leave the provincial fold. My brother, Kevin, thought it was time for me to move on. David Peterson and the Liberal caucus in Toronto did everything they could to encourage me to stay. I received calls from provincial caucus members and assistants. The Opposition House leader, Bob Nixon, said if he were in my shoes, he would make the move. I also had another personal consideration. That spring while on vacation in Florida I had met my future husband, Richard Marrero. Although at that point we had made no permanent plans, I very much wanted to hear his view of any political moves. Knowing neither Ottawa nor Toronto, he was determined only to support whatever decision I made.

I was torn, changing my mind almost daily about what I should do. My decision was sealed, ironically, by a plea to stay from the chairman of the Ontario Liberal campaign team. In a last-ditch effort to convince me not to leave, Ross McGregor came to my office in the north wing of the legislative buildings. Ross, who had managed David Peterson's campaign for the leadership, came directly to the point. "You know David Peterson will never be the premier. And if you stay, I will personally manage your next campaign for the leadership. But if you leave now, I will do everything in my power to destroy you."

That did it. I respond very, very badly to intimidation.

When I finally decided to run, the federal Liberals were substantially ahead in the polls. Although I believed the lead would not last, I nevertheless felt that we might salvage a minority government. After three and a half years in Opposition, I was ready to take the chance, especially since another women was prepared to run for my seat as MPP in Hamilton Centre. On July 10, 1984, I announced that I was leaving the provincial legislature to seek the federal Liberal nomination in the riding of Hamilton East.

It must seem to others, looking back, that I blew it. I left the provincial Liberals just before they came to power; I moved into federal politics just as the Liberal party went down to its worst defeat in Canadian history. Surely, you're asking yourself, she must be kicking herself? Not at all. If I had to do it again, knowing what I know now, I wouldn't change a thing.

To have the chance to play a part in rebuilding the national Liberal party is an experience I would not trade for any cabinet post. But the election campaign is one experience I would sooner not repeat.

It was the toughest fight of my political career. The former mayor, Jack Macdonald, had secured the Tory nomination for the riding of Hamilton East more than a year before the election was called. The NDP had nominated a union organizer named David Christopherson who could expect solid support in Canada's most industrialized riding. And many of the dedicated members of John

Munro's political machine were sitting this one out, disillusioned because their man had left politics and their party had rejected their choice for the leadership. In many ways, I was facing a repeat of my first election as a political novice back in 1977. Only this time, I kept in mind a few basic lessons.

My campaign team concentrated on the hometown theme. While many other candidates had launched their campaigns with the hope of capitalizing on the John Turner tide, I decided that in Hamilton East, I should stress the local angle. After all, their man, John Munro, had been defeated in the leadership; it would take some time for the party faithful to embrace our new leader.

I also realized that this campaign would be won or lost on organization. We had to get a good team in every poll and an election readiness group which would beat the opposition at its own game. It's said that in any federal election, the local candidate can only make a 5 to 10 per cent difference in the vote. However, in a tight race, that 5 per cent could mean the difference between victory and defeat. With an election team of more than 1,000 volunteers, we had to make sure that every last living Liberal supporter remembered to get to the polls on September 4th.

The NDP was known for effective election organization. Their access to union lists and union help has built a solid organizational base in most industrialized ridings. It was our job to out-organize both opposition parties.

At the beginning, our campaign seemed to be going straight downhill. The Liberals' original 16-point lead was being rapidly eroded as the national campaign strategy floundered. We were taking a beating in the polls and our door-to-door interviews revealed one overwhelming message: "We want the Liberals out."

Not only did the public want to get rid of the Liberals, but we seemed bent on self-destruction. Our campaign strategy was confused at best and sometimes downright embarrassing. As a local candidate, I decided to keep my head down and work. I was going to win the election in spite of anything going on around me. As for the national scene, we had to grin and bear it.

The national press reports were so bad we simply quit reading the newspapers. Shortly after the infamous bum-patting incident, I was being plagued by the press to give my view of the whole affair. What could I say? I didn't want to dump on my leader, nor did I want to condone any offensive body language. My response? Humour. "I am extremely disappointed. I met Mr. Turner recently and I thought I had a rather nice posterior but he didn't even go for it." The Toronto *Sun* carried that one as a local chuckle and it seemed to defuse the question. The challenge of boosting volunteer morale when the world was crashing around us wasn't easy.

Our own polls showed that our original lead — a handsome 10 per cent — was rapidly dwindling as undecided voters were opting for anyone but the Liberals. In our area, out of every six undecided voters, three were going to the Conservatives, two to the New Democrats, and only one was coming my way. We had to find a tactic, and fast, or we were in real trouble. But what would work? The answer came in the form of an invitation from then international trade minister, Francis Fox.

Throughout the campaign, we had been in constant touch with Fox's office, hoping to encourage him to come to Hamilton and explain the Liberal position on the issue of steel quotas. With two major steel companies in my riding, the voters were understandably nervous about increasing American protectionism. Fox was scheduled to come, but he discovered that (like most Quebec Liberals) he was in trouble in his own riding. He had to cancel our meetings in Hamilton. But he was prepared to meet in Washington to discuss the issues if I could fly down in 48 hours and join him while he attended trade talks at the US Department of International Trade and Commerce (ITC).

It was a gamble which I knew could backfire. But we needed something dramatic to pull us out of the downward spiral we were in. Maybe this was the way to do it. I went to Washington with another Liberal candidate from the Hamilton area, former MPP Eric Cunningham. We met with representatives of ITC, as well as the Canadian representatives, Fox and MP Ron Irwin. We organized meetings with individual Congress members and met with the national Democratic policy committee while we were there. We met Fox at the Canadian Embassy, and he invited us to join him at his press conference. In truth, we had no official standing and no reason to be on the platform. The Washington trip took place less than a week before the election, and Fox believed he was throwing us a lifeline.

The Canadian press corps in Washington was skeptical. Why should two Liberal candidates come to Washington and share the podium with the minister? Our visit did make the national news back home, but it also sparked questions about our motives. The potential backlash could be more devastating than doing nothing.

We returned to the riding only five days before the election. The Conservative candidate, joined by a number of union organizers aligned with the NDP, cried foul. They accused us of damaging delicate steel discussions for partisan purposes. In fact, nothing was further from the truth. Most of the contacts we made were only useful for fact-finding, and could hardly disturb the negotiations. On the Thursday night before the election I was scheduled to face my two major opponents in a television debate, which could make or break the campaign.

I suspected that my trip to Washington would be the focus of attack, a belief which was confirmed when our headquarters received an anonymous call from someone in the PC camp. The caller told us that my opponent would be pulling out all the stops, including accusing me of committing a criminal act by going to Washington. I hadn't realized that American law requires all representatives of foreign governments and interests to register before they could meet with Congress or the government. However, the law specified that the registration only applied to paid lobbyists, and quite clearly I was exempt — a fact which we made sure of. I went in to the debate, therefore, with the knowledge that we'd laid an ambush for my opposition.

About halfway through, the attack came: "My advisors tell me that Miss Copps committed a criminal act by going to Washington without a lobby licence." I was ready and waiting. "Obviously you do not understand American law, because if you did, you would realize that the law applies only to paid foreign lobbyists. In fact, it is no crime to fight for steel jobs. I have just been accused of committing a criminal act, and I would ask my opponent to withdraw or I will be consulting my lawyers because you have just slandered me." My opponent's jaw dropped and his face drained of all colour. No further mention was made of the Washington trip. When the television lights went off, he fled without a word about my alleged 'criminal activity'.

When I got home, undecided voters were calling the house saying they had decided to support me on the basis of that debate. Some Conservatives even ripped up their PC lawn signs. It was a gamble, but it paid off. I could have done nothing and hoped to survive the Tory deluge, but my trip to Washington showed the voters I was prepared to take risks and fight for their interests.

As the national campaign drew to a close, we knew that the Liberals would lose it. So our message to the voters was clear: Do you want another government backbencher or do you want an opposition member? You can have the best of both worlds. You can get rid of the Liberals, and you can have a fighter in opposition.

On the night of September 4th as we watched the votes come in, the initial reports were discouraging. I was trailing in the first six polls to come in. I had a sinking feeling in the pit of my stomach; I would have to begin another job search tomorrow. But as the night went on, our organization came through. In strongly Liberal areas our voters came out in droves; we had two or three times as many votes as the opposition. The more than 1,000 workers who had volunteered to get the vote out on election day had certainly done their job. When the final tally was in we had defeated both opposition parties by 2,700 votes.

9

Down But Not Out

Rule 9: It's easier to build from the bottom up

As the returns came in across the country, Liberals were absolutely devastated. Never in the history of the country had there been such a massive repudiation of the Liberal party. And in the back of our minds there was a nagging question that wouldn't go away: does this spell the end of the once-great Liberal Party of Canada? Ed Broadbent thought so. Having undergone his own political rehabilitation in the year leading up to the election, he began crowing about the demise of the Liberal party within hours of the overwhelming PC victory.

"We are the official Opposition," he stated, barely waiting for the body to grow cold before he started the autopsy. Broadbent thought that Canada would follow trends in many other western industrialized nations, and that the election would polarize national politics between left and right. He believed that this would leave no room for the centrist, progressive liberal view. And he further believed that the weakened Liberal party, still stinging from its public repudiation, would be in no position to mount the kind of opposition attack in Parliament for which the New Democratic Party had become famous.

Indeed, as the Liberal caucus began to consider its position, we found ourselves divided. How could we recapture public support? Some felt strongly that our best approach was to lie low and hope that time would heal our wounds. They believed that no Liberal attack in the first year of the government's mandate would be credible, since the government was still somewhat bound by a Liberal agenda and Liberal programmes. Others, particularly those who represented provinces with a strong NDP contingent, took the opposite view. We felt that the NDP would be breathing down our necks. It was critical — even imperative — that we move quickly to assert ourselves as the real Opposition.

Our debate in caucus was heated. There was a real sense among some of the newcomers, those who had never had the responsibility (or the blame) that accompanied ministerial prerogative, that we had to assert ourselves and throw the government off its own agenda. We were a loose-knit group. Some had been friends before, others had met for the first time after the election but we all had one thing in common: we feared the emergence of the NDP as perhaps a greater threat to the Liberal party in the long term than the government's huge majority.

Some of us had a lot of practice in opposition. I had worked in the Ontario legislature with MP Don Boudria, the outspoken member from Glengarry-Prescott-Russell, and we came to Parliament together. I had known John Nunziata from the days when he fought a tight race against Ontario NDP leader Bob Rae for a seat in the legislature in a by-election in York East. I knew Sergio Marchi, another vocal young member, from the days when he worked as a political assistant to cabinet minister, Jim Fleming.

But other Liberals were new to me. Brian Tobin was a direct but charming Newfoundlander who had raised the level of House debate to an art form. Another, Jean-Claude Malepart, a portly Quebec MP, emerged from government backbench obscurity to catch the hearts of *Quebeçois* in his fight for senior citizens' pensions.

It was a loose, unstructured group with a common theme. Our

job in the first six months was to embark on a 'search and destroy' mission to expose the Mulroney government for what it really was: a 'let's-pretend' quasi-Liberal hodgepodge which had no intention of keeping its election promises.

That meant attacking the government on the ground where it was most vulnerable. One of the key areas had to be patronage. Mulroney would have been less vulnerable had he not been at his self-righteous best on the issue during the televised leaders' debate. Turner had tried to put a good front on a spate of Liberal appointments just before the election, insisting that he had given his word and had to keep it. Mulroney turned that virtue into a joke as he waved a sanctimonious finger at Turner and roared, "You had an option." He tried to make Turner a laughingstock and claimed that his government would show a new way, a different way, because, indeed, he had an option.

In fact, a more revealing view of Mulroney's real attitude came in an off-the-record discussion on his campaign plane when he said about patronage, "There's no whore like an old whore." That was Mulroney's real message. It was clear to us then, as it has since become clear to the rest of the country, that the Tories were desperately eager to get their snouts in the trough. After years of opposition they wanted their beer and pickles. But Mulroney couldn't resist the temptation to look purer than Turner — an attitude which has embarrassed him ever since. No government is innocent of patronage but rarely has there been such a chorus of grunts and squeals from a front bench as occurred when the Mulroney government took office.

Patronage existed during the time of the previous Liberal government, but Mulroney raised it to a fine art. Cabinet ministers stood in line, palms out, snapping up the best jobs for sons, brothers, sisters-in-law and other friends and relations.

Day after day we rose in the House to compare the government's election promises to its performance. The aggressive tactics of some Liberal members did not pass unnoticed. Bob Hepburn of the Toronto *Star* wrote an article which zeroed in on four aggressive English-speaking Liberal members. He dubbed us the 'Rat Pack'.

A moniker can carry numerous connotations, not all of them positive. It wasn't our choice, it was his. But having been so named, we decided to adopt his title and to use the concept to the Liberal advantage. There has never been a conscious Rat Pack strategy, but our style was certainly in keeping with the image. We gnaw and nibble at the government, and we get at them in ways which they find hard to take. The artist husband of Liberal MP Therese Killens designed a logo for us, which we had printed on T-shirts that sold like hotcakes. We continued to mount an attack on government patronage and broken promises. For fun, we had a founding Rat Pack dinner where we established a rodent bill of rights.

The group named by Bob Hepburn included Don Boudria, myself, John Nunziata and Brian Tobin. Jean Lapierre and Jean-Claude Malepart were two other Rat Packers not mentioned in the English media.

The Rat Pack served two functions. We plotted together and collaborated on issues to pursue as a group in question period. But we also injected a shot of adrenalin into the caucus at a time when energy was badly needed. We supported our colleagues in the House with words of encouragement and applause. We heckled the government, and, in particular, the prime minister when his obfuscations in the House became unbearable. But we also managed to have some fun and inject some humour into a party and a caucus that was feeling rather humourless.

One of the things you learn early in politics is that you can't take yourself too seriously. There are too many battles to be fought.

If you don't keep your sense of humour, you lose all perspective on issues.

The humour was taken one step further when Liberal whip Jean-Robert Gauthier came up with an idea which epitomized our efforts. He suggested a patronage award of the week or 'PAW' award which would go out to the most deserving Tory — that is to the one who had gotten the best job that week.

We decided to launch our effort on a Friday morning. According to the existing standing orders, every member had a right to stand up and spend 90 seconds talking about any subject of interest. We agreed in advance that the first Rat Packer to be recognized by the Speaker would go ahead with the award. It turned out to be me. I rose in my place and asked Don Boudria, *à la* the Oscar awards, for "the envelope please". Don handed me the envelope on which were written the names of the nominees. I read them out and announced the winners, Peter and Marsha Clark, who could come to my office at any time to collect first prize, a Rat Pack T-shirt. The stunt (for so it was) won us a lot of Tory abuse, but it got our point across. But we didn't do it just to get public attention or to be funny; we did it for our caucus as well. We hoped it would lighten the atmosphere of intimidation we faced in a House dominated by 211 Conservatives.

I had no idea how overwhelming the numbers of government members could be until I arrived in the House of Commons and saw them spilling out on all sides, so numerous that they overflowed into our side of the House. When we spoke they could drown us out. A single voice, facing that kind of intimidation, can be swamped. You need support, applause and encouragement from your own colleagues — otherwise, you can't go on.

I remember the very first question I asked Mulroney in the House. The question dealt with the government's election promises regarding women, and the prime minister positively recoiled. He seemed surprised that I would even consider attacking him in such an aggressive fashion in the House of Commons. Clearly he was startled partly because he did not expect such aggression from a woman. But there were other reasons as well.

Brian Mulroney is a man who loves to be loved. He has built a career on a reputation for reconciliation, for mediation, for bridging both sides — in short, for being all things to all people. A classmate of his at St. Frances Xavier University told me that Mulroney's nickname at university was the 'yes man' because no matter what the group or issue, he always said yes. Likewise, fellow students at Laval have suggested that he was extremely popular because, no matter what the political viewpoint, people were always left with the impression that Brian was on their team. The socialists thought he was a socialist, the capitalists thought he was a capitalist, and (of course) the Liberals believed that he shared their ideals. Over and over during the election campaign I heard the same refrain: Brian Mulroney isn't so bad. After all, he's really a Liberal. In fact, he really is a chameleon; he has no particular political ideology or philosophy, but only a real need to blend into his surroundings.

Brian Mulroney was braced for armed combat with male members of the opposition. After all, he understood that the battle came with the territory. He was, however, totally unprepared for a similar attack from a woman. He simply could not understand why all the women of Canada weren't in love with him.

Instead of considering my questions seriously, he made comments about the level of my voice. He implied that somehow, because my voice was higher than those of my male colleagues, my questions were of less importance. But I stood my ground. I believed then, and still believe, that the prime minister fundamentally rejects the real equality of women. In time, the public, and especially women, will come to see the prime minister as I do.

74

You may remember that throughout the election campaign, some serious doubt remained about Mulroney's 'trust factor'. He was slick, he was glib, he had all the answers, but somehow they didn't quite ring true. He was not a man who could be trusted. It's interesting given 'feminine intuition', that fewer women than men voted for him. However, the trust factor was overridden by an even stronger desire to get rid of the Liberals. The public preferred the devil they didn't know to the one they did.

I was firmly convinced that the questions about Mulroney's trust factor would only grow with time, as the public came to know the man they had made prime minister.

The first public confrontation on the trust issue involved the question of universality. Mulroney had promised during the election that "universality is a sacred trust", but he was clearly preparing for an attack on universality as his first major political act. Two months after the election the government launched a trial balloon. Finance Minister Michael Wilson mused publicly that we might have to eliminate universality to pay off the deficit. His November economic statement suggested the possible elimination or reduction of family allowances and old-age pensions to some Canadians.

Brian Mulroney's promise about a "sacred trust" rang hollow in the face of these proposals. However, both opposition parties demanded that the government live up to its promise of universality. After persistent pounding in the House, the government was forced into an aboutface just before Christmas, which we all saw as a victory.

The November statement served notice that Brian Mulroney's pre-election promises may not coincide with reality. But it wasn't until the first budget that the truth about Mulroney's falsehoods really began to sink in.

During the election campaign in Sherbrooke, Quebec, Mulroney had promised that senior citizens' pensions would be exempt from any cutbacks. Yet the budget showed that every senior citizen would face a 3 per cent cut through de-indexing of pensions. The opposition began the attack in the House, but it was the fury of seniors that forced the prime minister to back down. The finance minister nobly offered to sacrifice seniors for the sake of their grandchildren. But he underestimated public support for our elderly. There's a sense, in our society, that seniors have earned their benefits, that they can least afford the ravages of inflation, and that we have a duty to fight for them. Their rights are the ultimate 'motherhood' issue. Above all, Wilson had forgotten the words of the prime minister, who promised during an election pep rally that he would increase all old-age pensions on January 1, 1985.

Seniors were angry and they had the support of the country behind them. A rally had been organized and busloads of them were arriving on the Hill. It was pouring rain, but about 200 joined the march. Throughout the demonstration, the mellifluous baritone of Brian Mulroney roared out over the crowd. No, he didn't attend the rally; the group had a tape of his infamous Sherbrooke promise to senior citizens. And they played the tape over and over again while they called for the prime minister and the minister of finance to meet with them. A group of seniors had met early in the day with our caucus and the caucus of the New Democratic Party, but Mulroney (most unfortunately) couldn't find time for them. When he refused their request, he failed to reckon with the likes of Madame Solange Denis.

She was 63 and all of about 80 pounds, but she muscled her way through a teeming crowd of reporters to confront the prime minister as his limousine halted in front of the Parliament Buildings. She asked him about his promise the previous summer in Sherbrooke. The prime minister was vague and conciliatory but Madame was taking no guff from him. "You promised and you lied. Well just wait until the next election, and it's goodbye Charlie Brown."

Every major newscast that night covered Madame Denis. Etched in the minds of the public was the phrase "Goodbye Charlie Brown." The government quickly backed off in an effort to minimize political damage. But the damage was already done. The prime minister's highly selective memory and his disregard of his own statements would haunt him in the months to come. We'd learned how far we could trust him.

10

I Say What I Mean and I Mean What I Say

Rule 10: In the long run, the truth never hurts

When I was growing up, I asked my father what was the key to success in politics. His reply may sound like a whole collection of platitudes, but he was right. Tell the truth and work hard. Luck comes to those who work for it, and it's more likely to last if you stick to the truth. Honesty may make you unpopular but lying, obfuscating, shirking or hiding will do more harm in the long run.

In politics as in life, one credo must guide your work: to thine own self be true. Long after people leave politics, they have to live with themselves and with the knowledge of how their political actions have helped or hurt the lives of others. Honesty may hurt in the short run, but in the long run people will respect your ideas. They may not always like or agree with them; but they will recognize that when you take a position, you do so because the position reflects your beliefs, not your polling data.

A certain amount of compromise is necessary in politics; no one has all the answers. But there must be a guiding belief which governs your life, with or without politics.

I grew up in a political family. From the time I was in grade four, my father was on city council, after years as an officer of the

Knights of Columbus. It was actually his principles that brought him into politics. He was first elected in 1960, the year that John Fitzgerald Kennedy became the youngest president and the first Catholic ever to occupy the office.

The then mayor of Hamilton, Lloyd D. Jackson, was about to retire, and there were fears that he would be succeeded by an aspirant who was known for his anti-Catholicism. The local Roman Catholic school board was in the process of acquiring land to build schools, and municipal opposition would be a real stumbling block. So a group from the Knights of Columbus got together to run a candidate who could best represent their views. They decided on my dad.

When my father ran for office, everyone got involved. My older sister, Mary, and I were walking to Brownies one night and we made up a song for the campaign. We came home and sang it to my parents. My father was bowled over and insisted the song would be a perfect kickoff to his campaign rally. We loved the idea. I was a born ham, and my sisters were keen to make a contribution.

I remember our first campaign appearance as if it were yesterday. My mother had sewn matching dresses in different colors for the three sisters. We all bounded on stage and began the song. We were barely into the first line when my younger sister, Brenda, and I burst into paroxyms of laughter. Mary was forced to wobble on alone as our political debut was drowned by giggles.

Our political education was largely conducted at the dinner table. Meal times at our house were (and still are) exercises in verbal acrobatics. My father was not the arguing type; his method was to throw out a provocative statement and sit back and chuckle while the rest of us fought about it. We discussed everything from the role of the church in the community to Sunday store-hour openings. There were no rules and no holds barred. At times, the only thing that prevented intelligent discussion was the ascending decibel levels of all concerned.

My political education outside the home was another story.

When my father was first elected mayor, it was 1962 and I was in grade six. The local newspaper wanted to come and take a family portrait, so for the first time in my life I was permitted to arrive late for school. When I walked into the classroom, my fellow students rose and applauded in unison. Why? I wondered. My father won the election, not me and it shouldn't make any difference in my life. But it did. Growing up in a medium-sized Canadian city (Hamilton's population is now 308,000) meant that the mayor's children came in for a certain amount of attention.

It was attention I could do without. That same year I worked very hard in a public speaking contest at my school which would lead to a competition sponsored by the local Legion. I won the competition and a chance to compete further. As I was given the award a competitor whispered, "The only reason you won is because your father is the mayor." I was devastated.

A similar experience in high school heightened my resolve for an independent identity. My father was going through one of the rites of passage for all politicians, the grilling that goes with the task of raising your own salary. A raise had been suggested for all council members. My father had rejected the hike, pledging to give it to charity, but a group of citizens paraded in front of city hall bearing placards reading 'Copps and the Robbers'. I had been given a new coat as a birthday present and when I proudly wore it to school, one of my classmates smirked, "Did you buy that with your father's raise?"

I had to grow a good, tough hide. I ignored the insults, but built a strong internal resolve that I would never do anything because "I was the mayor's daughter." If anything, as an adolescent, I rebelled against being a model student. Although I achieved fairly good marks and was actively involved in after-school sports and activities, I led the class in pranks and mischief. I was lippy. I would hurl insults at teachers on a regular basis — not to hurt them but to inject some levity into the classroom. I once lugged a spare inner tube into my Latin class so that I could distract the class by slowly leaking the air out of the tube while the teacher droned on. At school outings, parents were always happy to get their daughters to go out with me because I was 'respectable'. Little did they know that, once out of earshot, I would lead in the hell raising.

One night our school basketball team was invited to an out-of-town tournament. Before we left for the big weekend in Toronto, the vice-principal warned us that we should be an example to other participants. When we arrived, I decided to put a scare into some of the girls from our team who were staying in the next room. I removed the screen on the window and climbed out on the ledge, planning to scratch on their window and scare the bejesus out of them. It didn't bother me that the ledge was several stories high, but it did disturb passing pedestrians, who decided that I planned to commit suicide. A crowd gathered and began shouting, "Don't jump, don't jump." A few minutes later, I heard police sirens and quickly scuttled back to my room, where we awaited the men in blue. It was a little difficult to explain that I wasn't interested in self-destruction, but rather just wanted to play a trick on some fellow basketballers.

Hardly the stuff of delinquency. Although my mother surprised me recently when she claimed that, without her strong influence, I would have become a juvenile delinquent.

My experience in organized sports was a great preparation for politics. More young women should participate in competitive sports; the lessons learned on the playing field are so useful in the political arena. Even some of the terminology remains the same.

In politics, we talk about the scrum, where reporters move in on the player of the day. In free trade discussions, the US president talks about a level playing field.

Involvement in sports teaches you how to work as a team. It teaches you to accept defeat and to share in victory. It teaches you when to go all out, when to conserve your energies and how to learn from losing. The competitive edge honed in team sports also gives you a taste of life in politics. Competition is not something to be feared. It is something to be embraced and encouraged as long as you keep in mind that it is the means to an end and not an end in itself. There are times when the loss of an important game, the failure of an important play, can temporarily subsume your entire existence. But it is only in that experience that you learn to cope with winning and losing. Unfortunately, it is still too true that young women have not shared equally in the experience of winning and losing. I say that, not to assign blame, but so that we can realize we can't expect women to get out and run, to seek equal representation in Parliament until we re-examine our whole value system as it pertains to both sexes.

Our girls' high school basketball team was extremely successful. We won several championships and a number of us were in Canada-wide competition. In some years, our boys' team was not as successful. But, whenever a problem cropped up about gym scheduling, the girls' team was always expected to bow out and sacrifice our playing time.

I never considered myself political, or particularly interested in 'girls' rights', but I remember one visit to the principal's office to fight it out on this very issue. The girls were in the thick of a city-wide race for the pennant while the boys had unfortunately lost a chance at the championship. The school needed the gym for a school assembly, so it was decided that the girls would have to skip their practice. We had to battle it out with the principal, but we finally convinced him that we had every bit as much right to practice time as the boys.

Similarly, when you have won, you like to have the fact known. How many times would I read the paper or listen to the radio and hear the triumphs and travails of all the boys' teams across the city? How seldom would I hear the results of the girls' competition?

Obviously the lack of recognition will not make or break an Olympic athlete. But it is one way in which society validates competition among young men and boys, while downplaying those same efforts among young women. Then we wonder why women are more reluctant to compete, to take a chance, to expose themselves to potential failure on the floor of the House of Commons.

Those women who have shown that they *could* hold their own — people like Judy LaMarsh, Monique Bégin or Agnes Macphail — have been regarded as oddities. Their toughness was seen as an anomoly in some way; a denial of their proper femininity.

Look at the word itself. Aggression in men is considered a positive quality. An aggressive man will get out there and succeed. He will be a winner in business, in his profession, or in politics. The label is positive if you happen to be male. If, however, you are female and you happen to be aggressive you're considered shrill, a snarler, insecure with your feminity. You don't enjoy your womanhood and are somehow bent on castrating all men so you can finally be their equal. There's no sense of the positive about the label 'aggressive' when it is applied to a woman.

I don't know how many times people have told me that I'm not what they expect. "You're actually nice" they say, surprised. They have developed an image of me based on my work in the House of Commons and on media reports. And the image is shrill and aggressive.

Picture the House of Commons. It's a large room where you

speak to your fellow members in an effort to get your point across. At times, the atmosphere becomes heated. As a woman, my voice rises. A lot of men are loud, but my soprano carries over their baritones. It's pure physiology, a matter of the vocal cords. I don't know how many sarcastic comments I've heard from all sides about women's shrillness — comments relating not to the substance of the question or answer, but rather to its pitch.

A sing-song background mimicry is often the way that frustrated male members of the House will voice their discontent. Of course we should take criticism; that's part of our job. But to mock female members for their high voices is just plain childish. I dish it out and I should certainly be prepared to take it. But I believe we must get away from applying a double standard; one that says that aggression in a man is a quality to be admired but that aggression in a woman means she is giving up her womanhood.

Although there are more women in the current House of Commons than ever before, most of us lead very untypical lives. Compared to the national average, fewer are married. Among the men in Parliament, there seems to be the sense that a male politician must have a wife and two or three smiling children. The politician as provider, as father, as good family man. If you are a woman in politics, there is almost a sense of betrayal if your life includes anything or anyone else, including a husband or family. Margaret Thatcher's husband Denis catches a lot more flak than Mila Mulroney or Nancy Reagan. Poor Thatcher is caricatured as a wimp, a henpecked hubby, a man who hangs on his wife's skirts — even though he had his own successful career while his wife raised their children.

If a young man ascends the political ladder and successfully combines that effort with a happy family life, he becomes complete. If you are a woman, there is always the question, "How can you look after your children?" When Pauline Marois ran for the leadership of the *Parti Québécois*, the question of her family responsibilities dogged her at every step. Those same questions were not levelled at her opponent, Pierre-Marc Johnson, even though he too was a parent.

I will never forget a comment made when I was a member of the provincial legislature. One of my colleagues was talking about an MPP who bore a child during her term of office. He said he saw her hauling her child across the street, over to the legislature, with all the baby paraphernalia. She looked so exhausted, he felt sorry for her. She lost the next election and he attributed her loss to the fact that she just couldn't do both, be a mother and a member of the legislature.

When I married in the summer of 1985, I had already been working full-time in politics for eight years, yet an amazing number of people asked me whether I planned to quit my job. The unstated reason was that I had now snagged a man and should get down to the real business of womanhood, having babies. And everyone knows that babies and politics don't mix. In fact, until a group of members of Parliament headed by Pat Carney banded together after the election of 1979, politics and children didn't mix.

As a member of Parliament, you are entitled to fly back and forth to your riding a certain number of times at the taxpayers' expense. Your spouse is allowed to use some of these trips, in recognition of the fact that politics forces separation on you. Weekends may be your only chance to see each other. However, until the arrival of Pat Carney, no provisions were made to transfer the spouse's benefit to any other member of the family. Ms. Carney was a single parent with a teenage son living in Vancouver. Naturally she wanted to see him from time to time and to have him occasionally travel to Ottawa. The House of Commons refused. So Ms. Carney decided that she would go on strike, and refused to enter the House until a new ruling was made. Other women in the House joined her. It took only a few days to reverse the rule, and Ms. Carney could bring her son to Ottawa.

That was one of the few occasions when the women of the House of Commons rose *en masse* to defend their rights. All too often, we are tied by party discipline and party labels and we can't work together in a parliamentary democracy the way we should.

When we *do* put our collective political heads together, we can certainly make sparks fly. Remember the arrival of the new Constitution, back in 1982, with a Charter of Rights which was to enshrine such fundamental rights as the equality of women and the rights of our aboriginal people.

By 1982, we had more women in the House of Commons than when the British North America Act was originally drawn up: fourteen versus none. The second group of founding parents was, like the first, exclusively male. The prime minister and the premiers were charged with the responsibility for all major constitutional changes. When push came to shove, certain premiers were unprepared to embrace real equality, either for women or for aboriginal peoples.

Some Conservative premiers were vehemently opposed to the inclusion of a section protecting the equality of women in the charter. So the federal government, seeking consensus at all costs, agreed to delete section 28, which would have provided the guarantees that women across the country had been seeking.

That ill-conceived decision led to an explosion of all-party political activity, the likes of which I've never seen before or since. Impromptu meetings across the country were organized, and an all-party movement grew to put pressure on the federal government and provincial premiers to include overriding equality for women in the charter. The then federal minister responsible for women, Judy Erola, spearheaded the attack. Phone lines from her office buzzed across the country, informing, organizing and getting the message out. Likewise, representatives from such lobby groups as the national action committee on the status of women to Progressive Conservative Laura Sabia were heard imploring their male colleagues to wake up, grow up, and face the 20th century.

Etched in my mind was a meeting organized on very short notice at the Ontario Institute for Studies in Education in Toronto. The room was packed. The stage was peopled by more than a dozen representatives from across the political spectrum. Liberals, Conservatives, New Democrats and non-party women were there, seeking consensus on the most important political debate that would face our generation. Were we going to sit back and allow a couple of male premiers to railroad through a constitution which denied basic equality to the majority of people in our country? A resounding, "No." Were we prepared to act together as one, including all political parties, in an effort to force the new Fathers of Confederation to realize that we would not be denied our basic democratic rights? An overwhelming, "Yes." That night, telegrams went out, hotline shows buzzed, letters were sent, phones rang. For the first time in my memory we saw a political movement which overran party boundaries. Something unique was happening, so unusual that the women of Canada were able to convince our leaders that we would not be ignored. We would not be denied.

How did it happen? The pen may be mightier than the sword, but the ballot box is mightier than either. Politicians aren't fools; they know that they need support from the people to carry on their work. Manitoba Premier Stirling Lyon, who opposed the equality clause, had underestimated the power of public opinion. During the course of the constitutional debate he was defeated in a provincial election. The ballot box is the final judgment.

To those who were organizing in other provinces the message

was clear: when women get together, nothing can stop us. We succeeded in getting section 28 reinserted and we also drove home the point that no politician can ignore the wishes of the majority of the population and get away with it.

Why don't women work more closely together, regardless of political affiliation? I think it's because one of the strongest features of a parliamentary system is party solidarity. If you really believe that your chosen political philosophy is the best vehicle for social change, then your first job is to make sure that your political philosophy and party prevail. Whatever the political philosophy of her choice, a woman in politics must be convinced that her party can best embody positive social and economic changes. In a sense, the vehicle for social change is the party, not the gender.

Some women reject their responsibility toward the group by denying the very existence of inequalities — a phenomenon called the 'Queen Bee Syndrome'. It exists in politics as it exists in the real world. The classic Queen Bee has made it on her own and sees no need for the kind of sisterhood which gives each of us a collective responsibility to help other women. The Queen Bee did it with no one's help, and she cannot see why other women can't do the same. The Queen Bee cannot see what all the fuss is about. Since she succeeded without equal pay and better daycare, why can't everyone? She believes that the only thing holding a woman back is herself.

The Bee is a dying breed. Perhaps more insidious is the group of anti-feminists à la Phyllis Schlafly, who are lobbying to convince Parliament that they are the *real* women. They claim that equality is not necessary, and they fight against the social and economic progress that feminists seek. What they don't seem to realize is that feminism doesn't force everyone to work outside the home. Feminism seeks to offer a choice. It fights not only for equality in the workplace, but also for support for women who choose to work at home. Unlike the Schlaflys of this world, feminists realize that many women have no choice; they must earn their own livings.

I take pride in being a feminist. Look at the word itself; it comes from the Latin *femina*, woman; and being a woman is cause enough for being proud. I take pride, too, in representing my constituency — not only the riding which sent me to Parliament, but my larger constituency, the women of Canada. I am no more ashamed of representing their interests than Eugene Whelan would be of fighting for farmers. I can't understand how anyone, regardless of party, can think of women's issues as being trivial; what issues can matter more? Imagine my horror when I read a *Chatelaine* article about women in Parliament and found that a number of Conservatives proudly stated that they were not feminists. One even went so far as to claim that women's issues only made up one per cent of her riding anyway.

Then you face the curious situation where your fellow parliamentarians invoke feminism to avoid the truth. Some months ago I was criticizing Andrée Champagne. She had made national headlines when, in her capacity as minister of youth, she sent a letter defining her job as a potential recruiter of young people to the Progressive Conservative party. I stood in the House and called for her resignation. I felt she had failed in her responsibility to young people, by failing to fight for those in our society who were becoming part of a lost generation.

A few minutes later, I received a note from a Progressive Conservative member in the backbenches. This woman had written to berate me, saying women in the House must support all our female ministers. Because they are so few, they should not be criticized. Ironically, that same backbencher, Monique Landry, is now a minister while Andrée Champagne has been replaced.

My response to Landry: If a person, man or woman, is incompetent, he or she cannot escape criticism. Ministers should work for people they represent, and the opposition should hold the ministry accountable. Just as I will never criticize a female minister for the level of her voice, so I will never ignore her inadequacies just because she happens to be a woman. All we women want is chance to seek equality. We don't want special treatment, to be guarded from the realities of political life because of our gender. Nor do we want to be protected because we happen to be few in cabinet. Propping up is as bad as cutting down. Both say that women need to be judged by a different set of standards because somehow we are inherently weaker, less capable or less intelligent than men. I believe we are men's equals, and should be criticized or supported when we deserve it.

That is probably why I am one of the few politicians to have publicly criticized Mila Mulroney. Some months ago, I was called by a reporter and asked what I thought of the prime minister's wife. As is my habit, I tried to be honest. While I certainly respected her support for her husband and family, I could not entirely support her decision to drop a promising engineering career so she could fulfil her role as wife and mother. I said I would prefer Maureen McTeer as a role model for my children. I also said that I felt her adoption of the role of wife as political ornament had set the women's movement back by two decades. Criticizing Mrs. Mulroney is like criticizing apple pie.

But think of the criticism which followed Maureen McTeer's decision to pursue her own career and her own issues. Just what does that say about society's continuing perception of women? Maureen McTeer was pilloried and her husband was called a wimp.

She was painted as a scheming shrew because she had the courage to stick to her own agenda in the face of public opposition. How many women in the 1980s have chosen to keep their maiden name when they marry, as a gesture of personal integrity? Yet because she happened to be the wife of the prime minister, she came in for constant criticism.

Conversely, Mila Mulroney is praised, even named woman of the year, because she has obviously decided to devote her life's work to the advancement of her husband's career. Just what kind of message does that send to our children? It reinforces the notion that a woman's role is to support her spouse, while there is something underhanded and insidious about a woman who wants to develop her own abilities in her own way. Mila Mulroney's idea of working is to bring her baby's playpen to the office while she organizes and responds to her public duties as Brian Mulroney's wife. Needless to say, most women can neither afford a full-time nanny nor take their children to work with them.

I want my sons and daughters to be prepared for the independent roles they may be forced to play in real life. According to recent studies many girls still dream about marrying wealth and security. Few set their sights on specific careers which would give them financial security. Fewer still consider other, very real possibilities: that they might never marry at all, that a marriage could end in divorce, or that Prince Charming could be a sanitation worker, not a neurosurgeon. What happens if things go wrong? These young women have a romantic view of the world, and their view fails to include certain realities. In most major cities, a family needs two incomes to hang on to middle-class standards of comfort. Husbands

91

get laid off, or die, or leave. Unless these girls face up to real life, they will find themselves forced into a workforce for which they are singularly ill-equipped.

And there's another, more promising reality: they just might enjoy having a career. They might learn to take pride and pleasure in their work, as men have done for millenia. But to shoot for the moon, to be the best you can be, requires good role models, and all too often our role models are of the masculine variety.

We need to give our young women something to look up to, but first we have to break down the barriers of law and custom which keep women in their place. How can a girl aspire to command if she's not allowed to fight in the Armed Forces? What reward is there to being a first-rate nurse, or secretary, or childcare worker (all predominantly female occupations) when these jobs pay so little and have such low status? There are still too many obstacles for us to overcome. Yes, we want to be in the house where we belong: the House of Commons.

11

When A House Is Not A Home

Rule 11: Never ask a question unless you know the answer

If you took the name literally, the House of Commons should be a place where women feel very much at home. After all, this intimate chamber is supposed to be a microcosm of our country. Since women make up the majority, we should feel a part of the process in which 282 people meet to define, refine and reshape the laws of our land.

But from the moment you step inside, you sense that this place is foreign to women, alien to our spirit of cooperation, steeped in confrontation and simply not a place for traditional female virtues.

The very composition of the chamber lends itself to confrontation. The government traditionally sits to the right of the Speaker, the opposition to the left. The House is literally divided. At present, because of their overwhelming numbers, the Conservatives sit on both sides. The leader of the Opposition sits directly opposite the prime minister. The senior members of our caucus are opposite the major players in the Conservative cabinet. The traditions of the House create an atmosphere which is combative, not conciliatory; aggressive not consultative — a forum in which many women feel there is no place for them.

93

It's always been like this. Look at the paraphernalia of the House of Commons. The symbolic instrument which convenes a Parliament, the mace, was originally a medieval war club with a spiked head. The mace is now the ceremonial staff which must be present in the Chamber before any debate can begin. It is carried in by the sergeant-at-arms, who is also charged with the responsibility of ejecting any unruly member on orders from the Speaker.

The confrontational setting is hardly the atmosphere to encourage intelligent, non-partisan debate on issues which affect the life of every Canadian. It could, however, be argued that the House is not intended to provide a forum for non-partisan debate, but instead provides a place where government action or inaction can be debated on a daily basis by members of Her Majesty's Loyal Opposition.

One of the central components in this process is question period. Some argue that question period has deteriorated into a superficial, insubstantial attack on government policies that does not permit the public to understand the full process. Question period is only a small part of the process that makes our government accountable. But it is the most visible part, the daily equalizer that can even out the incredible odds created by a huge government majority (currently 208 Tories out of a total of 282 members). In the 45-minute question period, no Canadian can get a complete understanding of the workings of Parliament nor, indeed, of government. It's unlikely that even a parliamentarian, working fourteen hours a day in politics, ever completely understands the full complexities of government. The same problem probably faces a minister trying to master the intricacies of a single department. But those 45 minutes give Canadians a thumbnail sketch of the major political questions of the day. The questions, not necessarily the answers.

Our job in question period is to simplify the issues, to hold the government accountable, and in particular, to force the prime minister to live up to his election promises. If he fails to live up to those promises, people can only draw one conclusion — the

same conclusion that we come to every day when we square up
for battle in the House of Commons: the prime minister cannot
be trusted. He is not a man of his word.

You will recall that during the last election the issue of trust
troubled many voters. They definitely wanted a change, but they
weren't quite sure they could trust this smooth-talking boy from
Baie-Comeau who seemed to have no difficulty being all things to
all people. His charm and adaptability meant he could criss-cross
the country and seem to be at home with all — no mean feat in
a country divided by political, geographic and economic schisms.
Nothwithstanding his charm, he left each Canadian town with
one unanswered question: how could he promise so much to so
many with so little and still deliver? Or did he have no intention
of delivering? Have we been had?

The question of trust was the single most important Tory problem
during the last campaign. And it was more apparent among women
voters than among men. For some reason — call it feminine intuition — we weren't as easily bowled over by his Irish charm as
were our male colleagues. However one thing was sure. Women
wanted the Liberals out at all costs and if that meant taking a
chance on Martin Brian Mulroney, they were prepared to do so.

Once elected, the prime minister began to be called to account
for all his promises. And one of our jobs in question period is to
make sure that all of his 337 election promises are not forgotten.
We want to be certain that Brian ("you had an option") Mulroney
remembers exactly what he said about patronage. We want the
Canadian public to know the true Martin Brian Mulroney before
the next election rolls around.

Whether the issue is shakes and shingles or the publishing industry, free trade talks or universality, it is our job to knock the PM
off stride — to force him to reveal his true but hidden agenda.

My American husband is fascinated by question period. He had
never been politically active in the United States, and had paid
little attention to the workings of his Congress. But when he came

to Canada and saw the prime minister confronted daily on issues as wide-ranging as Canadian policy on apartheid and the universality of our social programmes, he became a QP (question period) addict.

For those of us in opposition, much of our working day is involved in preparing for and following up the daily grind of question period. The first meeting starts at 8:30 am. The group is called the tactics committee and consists of members representing four Liberal committees which cover social policy, government and finance, regional and economic development, and external affairs and defence. The caucus executive members are permanent appointees to the tactics committee, and all members who wish to ask a question that day are invited to the meeting. The committee's debate, headed by House leader Herb Gray, centres on the focus for question period. Whatever the issue, we have two possible approaches. Do we set the agenda by pursuing issues which we feel the government must address? Or do we try to examine issues which the press have already picked up and follow their lead, in the hopes that the combined effort of the press and question period will force a response?

Each approach has its drawbacks. If we merely ride piggyback on the press, we don't develop long-term strategies for selling the Liberal message. If we ignore the current issues of the day in hopes of setting our own agenda, we may be seen as irrelevant and out of touch, since the media like to link question period with the topical questions of the day.

The purpose of the meeting is to lay all possible questions on the table. Before it begins, we are provided by our research staff with a summary of the major press stories which have broken overnight. This permits us to see if there are emerging issues of national interest. As well, each member may have a particular question relating to their shadow cabinet position. Now is the time to speak out.

Once all the possible topics have been introduced, we debate which questions should be asked and in what order. The order is important because it sends a signal about our priorities as a caucus. For example, should a question on the increasing violence in South Africa come before the free trade discussions or vice versa? At the same time, we discuss what questions John Turner should ask. Sometimes we might want to suggest that he pursue one major question and stay away from another. In the early days of the Stevens affair we believed that it would be better for other MPs to pursue the question in the House, but as the evidence grew more conclusive he wanted to speak out. Sometimes we emerge from the meeting with a real clash of interests. Sometimes a possible question falls in two critics' portfolios and one wants to ask a question while the other does not. The discussion can be heated but the final discussion is left to our Solomon, House leader Herb Gray. It is up to Herb to weigh all the factors and to ultimately decide which questions are asked and by whom.

When Herb agrees on the dozen or so questions that will be asked that day, he advises us to begin working on the wording of our individual questions. If we plan two or three rounds on a given subject (rounds being turns at question period) we may form small teams and devise an approach which ensures that all aspects of a particular question are covered. If we have an issue that requires follow-up, we may arrange for two or three members to ask in sequence. The government might dodge the first question but can't avoid the follow-ups. The group also advises John Turner on what we feel is the most important question of the day for him, and that information is transmitted via his political assistant, Scott Sheppard.

For much of the rest of the morning, we may be involved with other responsibilities — committee work, interviews and constituency responsibilities. We cannot devote our complete attention to question period. Each member of Parliament has a budget which

provides four or five staffers to cover constituency and parliamentary responsibilities. In opposition offices, our staff is intimately
involved in the daily preparation for question period.

As we race between committees and the House, we may grab a
sandwich at our desk to prepare for the 1:15 pm tactics meeting.
Now the adrenalin begins to surge. The tension is particularly high
if you are working on a question for which not all the information
is in. If it deals, for example, with conflict of interest, the chance
for backfire is great. If your facts are not correct, the minister's
rebuttal is easy, and your own question could result in considerable
embarrassment for you and your party. The primary rule in question
period is simple: *Never ask a question for which you don't already
know the answer.*

At 1:15 pm, we gather back in the tactics room, which is part
of the fourth floor Centre Block office space occupied by Liberal
Leader John Turner. The purpose of this meeting is to try out our
questions on our colleagues before we take them to the floor of the
House of Commons. We literally read the main question aloud
along with the supplementary question, asking our peers to pick
holes in the content and to respond as a minister would to any
factual errors. We want to second-guess what the minister's response might be, to prepare each member for any possible answer
in the House.

This tactics meeting allows us to shift gears if new issues have
emerged. If there is a morning development in the free trade question, we want to be ready with the most up-to-date information.
Sometimes we will actually introduce new possible questions at
this point in light of changing information. Herb may also decide
to change the order of the questions. Although each question must
be submitted in written form and rehearsed before the committee,
flexibility is crucial. If a minister introduces new information in
question period that totally destroys any possibility for follow-up,
we must be prepared to move on to other areas without looking
as though our strategy has collapsed.

We learned that lesson early on, when, during the tuna affair, we had a particularly aggressive question period planned. John Turner stood up to fire the opening salvo. He asked for the recall of a million cans of tainted tuna. John Fraser, the minister responsible, retorted that he had just ordered the recall. We had not even considered this response, and we were left fumbling, with no follow-up until we could get our strategy back on track.

The boardroom where we plot is steeped in history. At one time, it was the cabinet room of Mackenzie King. Beautiful floor-to-ceiling oak panelling and a massive fireplace provide the backdrop for our intrigue. A motto is carved in wood above each doorway: "Long live the king." What most people don't realize is that the prime minister was not concerned about the fate of our titular head of state. It was his own political future he was immortalizing. King's influence also appears in grotesque but intriguing murals in John Turner's office which include pictures of King's mother and the dog to which he was so devoted. Legend says that Mackenzie King never wanted to tell a lie, so when his office was constructed, he had a special false door set up so that he could step outside when an unwanted caller arrived. He believed that this made it easier for his secretary to say, "I'm sorry, Mr. King has just stepped out." These are the surroundings in which each day we plot our current tactical and long-term political approaches to the role of opposition.

One result of the age of technology means that we are confronted with the daily reality of the 30-second news clip. Our political predecessors could, and did, take their time in debating long-term political change. We have to be brief. Some analysts scoff at this short-term response to the political exigencies of the day. But unless you can reach the greatest number of people with the most under-standable and memorable message, all the political vision in the world won't make a government work.

Before question period begins at 2:00 pm, each party furnishes the Speaker with a list of questioners and the order in which they will appear. Even though members jump up to be recognized, the actual sequence has already been set by the three House leaders. The official Opposition starts off with two questions followed by the NDP with one. Then each party rotates in turn, with the occasional backbench Conservative question thrown in for good measure.

In most instances, we stick religiously to the script which has been planned and revised since the early morning meeting. Our questioning usually parallels quite closely the tack taken by the NDP. If we discover that they are raising an issue which we had ignored, we may decide to change priorities in mid-stream and follow up on their line of questioning. If a particular attack seems to be working well, we may add additional questions and continue on one topic disregarding our earlier strategy. In most instances, people have been warned in advance to stand by for a possible follow-up question on a hot issue. However, in some circumstances, Herb Gray will decide to continue a specific line of questioning and he will call on certain pinch hitters who can be counted on to deliver a good question on just about any subject. One of those extraordinary members is George Baker, an MP from Newfoundland who can fire off a terrific question with only a few minutes notice.

It is during question period that the infamous heckling becomes most pronounced. As soon as I stand up to ask a question, I am usually met by a barrage of Conservatives crying, "Shh, shh, shh," in unison or commenting on my voice. The only way to deal with that is to ignore them. Absolute concentration is a must. When I am asking my question, the whole chamber could be collapsing around me and I wouldn't notice, because I am focusing on only one target: the minister in question.

When the minister responds, it is the opposition's turn to try to throw the government off stride. When ministers wander or obfuscate, we will interject with a heckle designed to bring them back to their job — answering the question. One thing that may surprise you: there is no rule that a minister must answer the question. He or she can choose to talk about the weather. But when this happens, we try to heckle them back on track. There are times, however, when heckling can work against us. It sometimes permits the minister, or the prime minister, to completely avoid the main question and to respond to the hecklers with snide asides.

It may sometimes seem that the opposition tends to latch onto headline-grabbing issues rather than confronting broader, long-term questions. This is partly true. It's easier for most Canadians to take an interest in abuses of power, for example, than in fiscal policy; and part of our job as opposition members is to bring the government's failings to public attention.

But some of the issues we bring up don't get much attention — at least, not at the time. When the government tried to limit senior citizens' pensions, telling those among the poorest in our society that they had to do their bit to reduce the deficit, all hell broke loose; but when the same government increased sales taxes so that a family earning $20,000 would pay an additional $592 in taxes each year, no one outside Parliament so much as hiccuped. People didn't respond in the same way because they hadn't yet seen the effect on their pay cheques. The fact is that most people don't complain until they actually get hit where it hurts, in the pocketbook. That is why it is so difficult to raise public awareness about the tax changes which are destroying the middle class. The government isn't crazy. It has instituted cumulative tax increases which will take about four years to filter through the system. By the time the taxpayers realize what has hit them, it will be too late.

Another case in point: for months after the government announced future changes to the Unemployment Insurance Act, we raised questions in the House and issued press releases to no avail. The changes meant that the unemployment benefits of a laid-off worker would be reduced by the amount of any pension he or she might be receiving. But in December 1984, no one seemed to care that in January 1986 a law affecting thousands of Canadian workers would be changing. Our letter-writing campaign to the minister continued but evoked very little response. But when these changes came into force in January 1986, there were demonstrations on the Hill and questions in the House; even some Conservative members publicly criticized the government.

When the demonstrators came to the Hill, we pounced on the minister inside the House of Commons. Flora MacDonald's response? This legislation was introduced more than a year ago, and we haven't heard a word about it. Why now? Opposition members had been raising the issue periodically for more than a year, but because the press had not caught on to the issue, the public was unaware of the change.

Sometimes a question can involve leaked information, which has arrived in an anonymous brown envelope. You may remember how the Liberals went after the minister of state for transport, Suzanne Blais-Grenier, for her wild spending spree in Paris and Stockholm at the taxpayers' expense. The information about the cost of Mme. Blais-Grenier's trip originally came to us through a request for access to information. Once a written request is filed, the government is required by law to produce any information within 30 days. However, the government provides as little information as is required by that law. In this case, we received the copies of all her hotel and limousine bills in unspecified cities. Since she had spent part of April in Paris, we calculated her limousine costs based on the French franc, but something just didn't seem right. It wasn't until 1:40 pm that day that we realized our mistake and were able to make the correct calculations, as the clock was ticking toward question period at 2:00 pm.

The former minister of state for transport tripped around Europe in a chauffeur-driven limousine at the taxpayers' expense, but people understood how her self-indulgence undermined the government's call for Canadians to tighten their belts. Brian Mulroney increased his personal staff by 54 per cent immediately after his election, and people realized that he had no intention of living up to his campaign promise of frugality. When the government spent more than $25,000 on limousines for a one-week prime ministerial visit to Paris, and when the prime minister was followed on his world tour by a second plane carrying his personal film crew, people also understood.

The Sinclair Stevens affair illustrates the group approach to question period. The *Globe and Mail* first broke the story by revealing that Stevens' wife, Noreen, had secured a $2.6 million loan for his company through contacts at a major Canadian company, which was simultaneously negotiating loans and grants through Stevens' ministry.

We were outraged when the minister claimed that he knew nothing about the loan and could see no conflict of interest. We formed a small working group, including Bob Kaplan, John Nunziata and our House leader Herb Gray, to explore all possible questions and to coordinate research on a daily basis.

The first week of questioning on the Stevens affair was a frustrating business. The press failed to pick up the story. The news of the Chernobyl disaster was eclipsing all other issues. We continued daily questioning in the House but the press did not seem to be interested. The NDP totally dropped out of the picture after a couple of fruitless days. Even in our morning tactics meeting, some members were suggesting that we drop the Stevens affair, or at least downplay it. We were adamant that the circumstances surrounding the loans were unethical and that the minister should resign. Each of us was researching the matter individually, as well as receiving information from outside sources. Once the press began to express an interest they, too, began digging up information. Then the NDP jumped back into the fray. The combined opposition assault, along with the discoveries by the press, ultimately led to the minister's resignation. But there were times during the episode when we never thought we would be able to force the issue to a head.

One incident in particular exemplified our frustration with the government's stonewalling policy. It's been nicknamed the 'chair-hopping incident', and it caught quite a lot of press attention.

The government tried to derail the Stevens scandal by shifting it from question period into committee — a tactic the Tories had used before with the bank fiasco. John Nunziata and I attended one meeting of the committee. From the moment Mr. Stevens walked in, it was obvious that he had no intention of dealing with any questions at all, whether about his personal finances or his involvement in the sale of Crown corporations like Canadair. He spent most of his allotted time showing us slides about the government's good works in conjunction with companies like Magna Corporation. Any questions concerning Magna's connection to the Stevens family finances were ruled out of order. The whole committee meeting was a farce.

As the committee chairman, who had deliberately blocked all debate, banged his gavel to end the meeting, I slammed my papers down in disgust and appealed to Mr. Stevens for an answer. We had to prove to the public that politicians are not crooks. John Nunziata walked up to Stevens and asked him to help clear the air. André Bissonnette, the towering minister of state for small business, grabbed John by the shoulders and pushed him out of the way. I wanted to confront Mr. Stevens, but the crowd around him was too thick, and I didn't want to jostle my way past the press cameras. I detoured around the side of the room, heading for the door, where I could position myself to meet Mr. Stevens as he left. Because of the crowd, the only way I could reach the door was by stepping over chairs.

As I neared the door and jumped down, Stevens came through, preceded by a flying wedge of bodies including the formidable Mr. Bissonnette and two assistants. One assistant shoved me up against the wall to keep me out of the way while Stevens left. I followed the group, begging the minister to clear up the scandal. Stevens ignored me and jumped into his limousine, leaving Mr. Bissonnette holding the bag. So much for ministerial accountability.

But the incessant pressure of questions ultimately succeeded. The Stevens affair had two casualties, since deputy prime minister Eric Nielsen's stonewalling tactics ultimately led to his demotion. He was relieved of his office after being seen as largely responsible for the escalation of the whole mess. If we had not persisted, it is likely that Stevens and Nielsen would both be ministers today.

One myth about Parliament must be demolished immediately. No politician of whatever stripe has all the answers to social and economic problems. Perrin Beatty, after moving from opposition to government said it was much easier to govern from the opposition benches. He is right. It's also fair to say that in any given 24 hours, the focus, the action, and the parliamentary agenda for 23 of those hours is set by the government. The government orchestrates all the daily business in the House of Commons, except for question period. The government essentially determines what bills become law. It assigns priorities to individual bills. It decides to set up a parliamentary task force or to take action through legislation. The prime minister can commandeer the airwaves to get his message across. His ministers can make the news by announcing new initiatives which they may have been preparing for months, while their opposition critics may only see the results as they are being handed out to the press.

It is no accident that when the House rises for the summer break or Christmas or Easter recess, the government's popularity rises. It is also no accident that when a government is in serious trouble, it takes refuge by temporarily dismissing the House. Without question period, the government controls the entire agenda and the flow of information comes only from the ruling party.

Some critics argue that a move toward an American-modelled congressional system would be a step in the right direction. They prefer the loose-knit and shifting alliances that occur in a system where party solidarity and party discipline don't always apply in voting patterns.

I am among those who believe that the system of party discipline has served our country well. If the current president of the United States had been forced to face the daily assault that governments undergo in the House of Commons, he would have been a one-term wonder. Instead, Ronald Reagan controls the agenda and the flow of information from the White House, unfettered by any legislative accountability to the Congress, 24 hours a day. His country sees less of the confrontation of philosophies and ideas

106

that face Canadians every night on the televised reruns of question period.

The daily grind of question period permits Canadians to see their leaders in an intimate fashion which is denied to the American public. We watch to see how the prime minister reacts under pressure, how the opposition mounts an attack and how individual ministers understand and keep up with their portfolios. No such opportunity exists in the United States, where the separation of the congressional and executive branches leads to isolation on both sides. That isolation also permits the American president to control aspects of the government's message. He chooses when to meet the public and how to do it. He can control his public persona completely, as a prime minister cannot.

The American system has its attraction, but the parliamentary system has some real strengths. Voters can judge you on the complete performance of your party, rather than simply considering issues as they arise. The American system has led to a situation where members vote all over the map, depending on the needs and wishes of their individual constituencies and the strength of political lobbies. In Canada, at least we understand that the party as a whole is the bottom line.

Only in the one hour of question period do the opposition and the private members control the agenda. That one hour includes fifteen minutes for private members' statements and 45 minutes for question period. Our job in opposition is to seize that single chance to get our message across — to expose the government where it's wrong and to encourage it to move in the right direction.

12

We Stand On Guard For Thee

Rule 12: Canada has a price worth paying

Aside from generalized mistrust of Brian Mulroney, the second theme that haunts the Mulroney government is an underlying fear that he is prepared to sell our country out. This fear was first exemplified by the diplomatic fiasco over the voyage of the *Polar Sea*.

It was the summer of 1985. The September slump had not yet hit the Tories, and most politicians were basking in the summer lull that usually means a rise in public opinion polls by the governing party. Rather than enjoying the temporary respite, External Affairs Secretary Joe Clark and his nemesis, Brian Mulroney, embarked on a collision course which could only end in embarrassment and confusion on all sides. The *Polar Sea* incident made Canadians begin to question the leadership of our country — a doubt which can only be exacerbated by the prime minister's further actions.

The United States government sent one of its ships, the *Polar Sea*, on a shortcut through Arctic waters. The waters in question are Canadian, but the Reagan administration failed to ask the Canadian government's permission before the ship sailed. Our government's response was confused at best. The prime minister said he didn't mind in the least; the minister of external affairs said he did.

The incident would almost have gone unnoticed except for a small band of nationalists led by Mel Hurtig, founder of the nationalist Council of Canadians movement. When the government failed to act, the group decided to draw the attention of the Canadian public to the invasion by hiring a small plane to fly over the *Polar Sea* and drop a Canadian flag wrapped in a mail tube onto the ship. The mission involved two university students who had never been involved in any protest activities before. The press was notified and all eyes were upon the small plane as it flew over the *Polar Sea*. The first and second attempts were unsuccessful; the flag landed in the sea. Finally, on the third try, the flag landed on the deck. Mission accomplished. The plane returned to civilization, photographer's flashes and the glare of publicity.

How did the government react to the *Polar Sea* incident? There was no formal protest to Washington over an invasion of our Arctic waters. But the government so misread public opinion on the issue that the Department of Transport decided to lay charges against the pilot of the plane, who was charged with flying too low and dropping a dangerous object. Since when has the Canadian flag been a dangerous object?

This incident illustrates the Mulroney government's inability to say no to the United States. Those Canadians who protested a violation of our territorial waters were punished while the offending trespassers got off scot-free. The *Polar Sea* incident was a precursor of the government's continuing failure to exercise its role as a separate and sovereign entity, an honest broker in an increasingly troubled world.

The prime minister himself often brags about his first job, singing for his supper to the head of an American-based multinational corporation. It seems that he expects the whole country to join his song. This shouldn't be surprising when we understand the roots of the man who is now leading the country. He's not ashamed of the Schefferville solution — shutting down an industry and paying off its workers as the answer to ongoing economic problems in Baie-Comeau.

The *Polar Sea* signalled the increasingly subservient relationship that would be reinforced by Mulroney's Shamrock Summit. The prime minister's recent trek to Washington for talks on acid rain, which deteriorated into a public relations exercise, is another such sign. This shows what happens when you put all your eggs in one economic basket.

Canada used to be a world leader in foreign policy. It used to be respected for its willingness to break from the Washington line when Canadian or global interests were better served by the breaking. We're rapidly losing that stature. When Corazon Aquino succeeded to the presidency of the Philippines, the Canadian government was unprepared to move until it got the okay from Washington. What happened to the Canadian peace initiatives begun by Lester Pearson and continued by Pierre Trudeau? We used to be a nation which set its own standards — witness the recognition of China and Cuba. What happened to the sovereignty of our great country?

I underline this theme because I believe that, while most Canadians jealously guard our role as an honest and independent intermediary, women are particulary involved and committed.

Women have taken a leadership role in peace initiatives. Perhaps our abiding concern for peace has to do with our biological investment in the future. Because we have been charged with the primary responsibility for raising children, we understand the world's vulnerability. We have never been weighed down by the respon-

110

sibility for fighting wars, so possibly we can see the peace issue more clearly.

Perhaps it's because our minds are less apt to be fuddled by the fumes of glory. We don't believe that any abstraction is worth the burned or broken bodies of children. Men may call us unrealistic, but possibly we're more practical. We too understand honour, duty, glory, freedom — all the concepts which men go to war for. But we see them in terms of life, not destruction — and we know who would have to clean up the mess left by the death-and-glory boys.

For whatever reason, women in Canada respond strongly and directly to the question of Canadian commitment to world peace. It is for this reason that I believe the prime minister is particulary vulnerable among the women of Canada.

As members of the opposition, it is our job to expose the short-sightedness of Canadian government policies, including the Con-servatives' unwillingness to develop independent foreign policy and the government's dependence upon the United States for economic recovery. Our opportunities are ample. The first is question period. Members charged with a certain responsibility (for example, foreign policy) form what is known as a shadow cabinet. Because there are so few of us, the entire Liberal caucus constitutes the shadow cabinet, and we also have the opportunity of getting involved in other dossiers. I am the Liberal critic for labour and housing but I am also the deputy health critic and vice-chairman of the standing committee on human rights. I am also chairman of the Liberal social policy committee, and I sit on the Liberal committee on free trade headed by Lloyd Axworthy. With all these irons in the fire, it is up to me to pursue issues in the House of Commons during question period, and out on the hustings.

A typical week for me would involve committee work and several speeches in the House, as well as speeches in the community. Some of the latter may be at Liberal events and others to the community at large. I may be invited to St. John's, Newfoundland, to speak to the Board of Trade or to Prince Edward Island to meet with the Zonta Club. I may meet with the Liberals in Penticton, BC or Yellowknife, NWT. Wherever I go, I emphasize the themes which I feel touch the hearts and minds of Canadians. Can Mr. Mulroney be trusted? Will there be a Canada left to fight for? These themes, it seems, reach Canadians from coast to coast. While there may be serious regional disparities, while people may be passionately loyal to their regions, all Canadians are concerned about the future of our country. Few Canadians believe that Brian Mulroney will best protect our interests.

John Turner's message is simple but true: "It may cost us a little more to be Canadians, but it is a price worth paying." Canadians see our neighbours to the south as our greatest friends. But our country has been built on different dreams — a fact which the Conservative government led by Brian Mulroney doesn't seem to understand.

Indeed, in the discussions surrounding free trade, Mr. Mulroney can't understand what all the fuss is about. Setting aside the potentially disastrous economic consequences, Canadians have expressed very real concerns about our cultural sovereignty. If we are pressured to negotiate away our uniquely Canadian health care and social programmes, will the next step be an economic union? If we are forced to revalue our currency to move closer to the American dollar, will we soon be seeking a single currency?

I think Canadians know the answers to those questions, but I don't think the prime minister does. His whole life has been built on subservience to American corporations. He's a company boy from a company town. But in this case, the town is Canada and the boy is the prime minister.

The issues to stir the imagination of Canadians are certainly there. And the interest is there. Why then, have so few women chosen to take up the challenge and enter public life? Why is it that even today, university and college campuses are teeming with young male politicians and the number of women who get involved in student government is still pathetically small?

Women understand the issues. We are concerned about the very existence of our country and our planet. Yet we seem content to allow the decisions which shape our future to be made without our involvement. We continue to play wallflower when it comes to changing the shape and directions of our lives.

13

Yes, You *Can* Make A Difference

Rule 13: Woman's place is in the house, and that's where she should go just as soon as she leaves the office

How many times have I knocked on a door during an election campaign only to be told, "I don't vote. It doesn't make any difference anyway." More often than not, if only one member of the household votes, it's the man of the family. Women will often say, "It's up to my husband," or, "I vote the way he does. We don't want to cancel each other out."

It is difficult to convince the sceptics that your vote is important, but consider this: in 1923 one vote gave Adolph Hitler leadership of the Nazi party. That fact underscores the importance of a single vote. But for that vote, the whole course of history might have been different. But it's difficult for each of us to see how a vote makes a difference in our daily lives.

Why is it so important that women begin to recognize the power of voting? We are the majority in this country, and yet in many instances we have left the political process to our male colleagues. Perhaps we think voting doesn't make a difference. But if so, why did the leaders of our three major political parties feel that women's issues were so important in the past election that they warranted a special debate? Not, one suspects, out of the kindness of their hearts.

More likely, the politicians were closely watching the phenomenon of gender voting as it has developed in the United States. Some would argue that in a disciplined party system there is no room for gender voting, since issues are not decided on their own merit but as part of a collective package upon which the voters must decide. But the majority of voters don't belong to a disciplined party system; they vote as they think best.

One only has to examine the political agenda for the 1980s to realize that women's issues are overriding questions that face each and every Canadian family. 'Women's issues' is a misnomer, since most issues concerning children and the family concern men as well as women. For example, why is daycare considered a women's issue? It concerns the whole family. Are schools a women's issue?

These are not women's issues, but issues of equality. Since women tend to be the losers in the area of economic and social equality, these concerns are lumped together under a trivializing heading, perhaps in the hopes that they might go away.

The first quest is that for economic equality. Women across Canada who work outside the home earn an average of 64 cents for every dollar earned by a man. We know that government cannot solve the problems of economic equality as long as the labour market undervalues the work of women. What, then, can government do to help bridge the gap?

Three crucial issues are involved in the march toward equality: employment equity, education and daycare. The first measure is the move toward equity. Before the Abella report, employment equity involved a number of initiatives including equal pay for work of equal value and affirmative action. Appointed by the Liberal government to analyse the problem of labour market inequalities between men and women, Judge Rosalie Abella suggested

115

that the package of initatives would be better understood under
the general heading of employment equity. Just what does employment equity involve?

The first element is equal pay for work of equal value. Equal
value does not mean equal pay for equal work. Equal pay for equal
work legislation has been in existence in most Canadian provinces
for more than three decades. It means equal pay for jobs of similar
worth. It is based on the principle that salary scales are subjective
assessments based on a number of variables. The number and types
of criteria vary, but most models include skill, effort, working
conditions and responsibility. The idea is to compare jobs within
the same company using these four criteria. By assessing these
variables, and no others, a company should be able to develop a
wage scale which is free of any gender bias.

Sound complicated? It isn't really. All it means is ignoring gender
when you decide on salaries. You may find it hard to believe that
current salary scales build in a bias for gender. But let's look at the
teaching profession as an example. When most teachers were women,
it was an underpaid, undervalued profession with little status. It
was only when men began entering in greater numbers that we
saw the salary scale and the social status of the teaching profession
improve.

You may argue that women have not occupied most professions
for long enough to garner the better-paying positions. But let's
look at the nursing profession. Across Canada, nursing is dominated by women. Men make up only 2.8 per cent of the nursing
profession, but they manage to secure a disproportionate number
of positions in nursing management, as hospital department nursing
heads and otherwise.

Pay equity legislation will not change the wage disparities between men and women overnight. Nor can it address the problem
of male-oriented promotion. But it will allow us to evaluate discrimination in concrete terms. It would give us some ground for
taking action when certain jobs done by men are overvalued and

116

jobs occupied by women are underpaid. The federal government instituted equal value laws in 1978. Although the system is far from perfect, five group salary awards totalling more than $20 million in retroactive pay have been negotiated with Treasury Board during this period. One case in point: a group of women nurses in a federal penitentiary were being paid less than male orderlies who had much less education. Equal pay for equal work laws did not protect the nurses since the work was similar but not exactly the same. It wasn't until the introduction of federal laws for equal value that these nurses could seek redress and salary increases.

But federal labour laws cover only 10 per cent of the population. Most provinces have not yet introduced equal value laws. We still find ourselves in the ridiculous position where a university librarian is paid less than a gardener.

Any change in equal value laws would result in only a marginal increase in women's salaries. A conservative estimate says the increase would be in the neighbourhood of 7 to 10 per cent. A 10 per cent salary increase is not to be sneezed at if you earn so much less than your male counterparts.

New legislation should include the notion of affirmative action. Affirmative action means that employers should give special consideration to hiring those who might otherwise be overlooked — women, visible minorities and the handicapped. How many times has a woman been refused a job because a prospective employer is convinced that she will get pregnant, or she will miss work because of her 'monthly problem', or her husband will be transferred to another city?

It is clear that some employers are still reluctant to hire women because of misconceptions about reliability and attendance. An affirmative action plan would balance out that prejudice. Discrimination has occurred, and continues to occur, against women in the marketplace. To balance this, an affirmative action plan would mean that (all else being equal) the woman will be given the job.

Reverse discrimination? You can think of it as a pendulum. When it swings too far for too long, sometimes it needs a push in the other direction.

Affirmative action can be carried out in a number of ways. The current federal government prefers the carrot approach: affirmative action should be voluntary, and companies should be allowed to choose their own timetables. The problem with this approach is that experience shows that few, if any, employers will bite. Their primary responsibility is to the bottom line, and they perceive externally imposed criteria, like affirmative action, as an interference with profit. (Most companies were not eager to outlaw child labour or adopt the minimum wage either.) The second approach is known as contract compliance. This method also leaves it up to the company to adopt affirmative action, but the carrot is juicier. If you do business with the federal government you must develop an affirmative action programme in order to qualify as a bidder for government contracts. This approach is an attractive one since it gives employers some leeway but includes an economic incentive. The third possibility, one which has not been embraced by the mainstream, is mandatory affirmative action with quotas which must be enforced. Judge Abella rejected this option in her study; she felt that we should first try voluntary compliance. Abella warned, however, that if we don't see progress in economic equality for women through a combination of employment equity initiatives, we may have to consider quotas in the future. In other words, quotas if necessary but not necessarily quotas.

The second question which faces all women seeking economic equality is the issue of education. How many times have you heard that women are paid less because they avoid math and the sciences and stick to the humanities? Granted, the more female doctors, engineers and scientists we have, the better. But careers such as these demand university education, usually at advanced levels. It is also unclear whether male-dominated professions like engineering would see a drop in salary level and prestige if they were suddenly invaded by armies of qualified females. While engineering is certainly a non-traditional field that holds promise for women, many other traditionally male jobs are not necessarily more challenging or beneficial than undervalued 'female jobs'. Should women be moving in droves to non-traditional jobs, or should we start re-evaluating the wages of assembly-line workers compared to the salaries paid to college graduates in early childhood education?

The fact is that Canadian women are no less educated than Canadian men. Most studies show they tend to be slightly better educated. Societal bias and economic norms have established that predominantly female jobs are worth less money than predominantly male ones. The law of the marketplace, you could argue. But if we truly believe that discrimination on the basis of sex is illegal, if we really support the constitutional amendments which give equal opportunity to men and women, then we should be prepared to embody these beliefs in law. That's all that we seek. Not a special deal, a better deal, nor an easier deal, but an equal deal.

That deal involves certain legislative changes to guarantee pay equity. But it also involves a social contract with our families. If we really expect women to have an equal opportunity in the marketplace, then we cannot continue to ignore, underemphasize and downplay the incredible need for adequate child care in this country. It's not just daycare. Daycare could probably continue to be provided in the haphazard, unequal and expensive manner that it is at the moment. But if we as a society embrace the notion of both men and women working outside the home, we must make a collective decision about what's happening to the children.

The last generation has seen a revolution in the involvement of women in the working marketplace. The majority of mothers are now holding down two full-time jobs: raising kids and working outside the home. We also know that the most important years for any growing child are between birth and age three. Yet it is a crying reality that daycare facilities for children under the age of three are expensive and limited.

If it is available, the cost of the service excludes most middle class families. That means access to organized, equipped daycare for young children is restricted to the very rich and professional couples, or to the very poor, whose costs are subsidized. Those in the middle are often forced to leave their children in inadequate surroundings and, in some cases, with little supervision or none at all.

I recently spoke with a Toronto area social worker who recounted the story of a single mother she represented in a dispute with the Children's Aid Society. This woman, an immigrant labourer, normally left her three-year-old with a regular babysitter. One day, the babysitter fell ill. Unable to make any other arrangements, and fearing the loss of her job if she failed to go to work, the woman left the child alone and phoned from work every hour to check in. At one point, the landlady saw the child playing alone and called the police. The child was taken from the mother and the local CAS made application for permanent wardship.

When these events were recounted in court, the judge ruled that the mother should retain custody. He said it was society that should be in court. Society so undervalues child rearing that we have no mechanisms for dealing with this sort of situation.

A two-year study on child care was recently tabled in the House of Commons. The Cooke Report, commissioned by the previous

Liberal government, called for public investment to the tune of $6.3 billion to develop a nation-wide system of early childhood education which would guarantee equal access for all. The response of the (largely male) press gallery was amazement: these irresponsible feminists could consider a $6.3 billion expenditure at a time when we are facing mounting pressure to reduce the public debt? But no one challenges the billions of dollars that are spent annually on the school system; everyone accepts (as they should) that all children should be educated from age five at the public expense. Nobody cries foul at a public education system which taxes all Canadians, with or without children, to pay for an education system which benefits all Canadians.

If we recognize that children are our greatest natural resource, that the years from birth to three are the most important in any child's life, and that working women are a fact of life in the 1980s, then surely we have a public responsibility — if not to working women, then at least to the children. Accessible, available and effective child care is the right of every Canadian. This is simply enlightened self-interest. If we don't provide for our children now, why should they pay for our pensions in 2010?

Is universality in daycare radical thinking? Given current political trends, perhaps it is. Again, if Parliament more accurately reflected Canadian society — that is, if we had more women, with or without children, working in Parliament — then we might see more sensitivity to the bread-and-butter issues that make a real difference to equality of the sexes.

Without adequate daycare, no working mother is really in a position to compete equally in the marketplace. Job equity and affirmative action may secure her the promotion she wants, but she won't be able to accept it unless she can go to work secure in the knowledge that her children are being well cared for. Anything less is mere lip service to the notion of equality. And heaven knows, we women don't want more lip service.

14

The Spirit is Willing

Rule 14: The flesh is never weak

So you want to be a politician. You've been bitten by the bug and would like to get involved. What do you do now?

There are a number of ways to start out. The most traditional is to join the political party of your choice. But if you are like many people, you may not know all that much about the parties. What differentiates a Liberal from a Conservative from a New Democrat? Just how do you decide on a political party anyway?

In my own case, my father had been a Liberal and, although I had not been politically involved, I had voted Liberal in the past. The Liberal riding association asked me to become involved. In many cases, it is something as simple as being asked.

When I first joined the Liberal party, I wondered secretly whether I was not really a closet New Democrat, since some of their views seemed to fit some of my concerns about equality. But it wasn't long before my work in the Liberal party convinced me that I had made the right choice. (Expect some prejudice: I am a Liberal by conviction and will support the aims of my party, so you must take my assessment with a grain of salt.) What I love about the Liberal party is its diversity; its members don't require conformity for success.

As a political philosophy liberalism combines the best of the collective and the individual. Liberalism is prepared to reward the spirit of individualism — heaven knows any party which can support William Lyon Mackenzie King and Pierre Trudeau must have some use for strong individualists. But our philosophy is underscored by an abiding belief that individual rights do not override the rights of society. The survival of the fittest has no place in a modern society which takes its collective responsibilities seriously.

Conversely, liberalism is never so tyrannized by the collective as to sacrifice individual rights. Recently, I read in the paper that two members of the New Democratic Party had been expelled because of their views on funding for separate schools in Ontario. I disagree utterly with their views, but I would defend to the end their right to dissent.

A great party can reconcile such differences, whether in caucus or in the party itself, and this is just as well because in a country as diverse as ours there are bound to be differences of opinion. What is a party if it cannot encourage diversity of views and internal debate? Therein lies the strength of the Liberal party. We will always have internal differences on a variety of issues, from multiculturalism to the management of our economy. But this heterogeneity is a strength not a weakness; our diversity is a source of ideas for the future. We will not tolerate the tyranny of the individual *nor* of the collective.

Suppose you haven't made up your mind about which party you might support. The best way of getting your feet wet is not by joining a party, but by involving yourself in a political battle. The issue doesn't have to be earth shattering. It could be something as small (but important) as the installation of a stop light on a killer corner in your neighbourhood. Set yourself an achievable goal: getting a stop light installed before the beginning of the next school year. Then marshall your resources. Who would be interested in the problem? Parents involved with the local home and school association, neighbourhood businesses, homeowners in general. Set up a public meeting. Get some publicity through newspapers, radio and television, so that your neighbours know about the meeting. Find out which of your municipal officials could influence the installation of the light and call them. The support of local school trustees could be critical. The school principal could give you some ideas about other players. Municipal aldermen should be involved. Enlist the mayor's support if you can. The more people you include on your team, the fewer will object to your request for the stop light.

Garner your support and keep everyone involved. The more information that you make available to the community, the greater your chance for success. Make sure all meetings are open and accessible. Communication is the key. Enlist the interest of the local media. If the newspaper feels your fight is worth a story, it will reach thousands, not hundreds, with your message.

Keep everyone informed, in writing. Take around a petition in a door-to-door canvass and keep the neighbourhood informed. Let the politicians know, in writing, how many people support your cause. Encourage local residents to write individual letters to their politicians at city hall. A single, handwritten letter has more impact than dozens of signatures on a petition. Above all, keep everyone informed and make them feel involved every step of the way.

Eventually you go to the traffic committee at city hall. You may or may not win, but you've learned what politics is all about. Moving from a battle over a stop light to a municipal election is not as difficult as it seems. You have already developed a network of friends and supporters. Many of them didn't know you before the battle of the stop light, but they may be your future political allies. Above all: don't be afraid to ask for help. When I first ran for election in 1977, I called every single living, breathing relative and friend I could remember. (It's a great reason to throw a family reunion.) Some refused outright, some were busy and some were of a different political stripe. But without exception, they were pleased and flattered that I took the time to call them personally. I didn't restrict my calls to members of the Liberal party. I phoned not only the undecided but also some who I knew belonged to other political parties. A few of the latter actually turned out to help; others promised not to work for my opponent but concentrated on other ridings in their provincial election work.

The principles involved in winning an election, whether for dogcatcher or member of Parliament are simple. You must develop an absolutely topnotch grassroots organization which will get you into the kitchen of every house in every neighbourhood in your ward or riding. Plan what you have to do, who you should see, where you should be, and set up a timetable. Stick to it. Try to get nominated early — you need all the time you can get. Organize coffee parties, which permit you to meet in the relaxed, informal atmosphere of a neighbourhood where you can chat about problems over a plate of cookies.

If you are seeking a party nomination, don't be daunted by the party establishment. In all three major parties, women tend to be nominated in no-win ridings. In winnable ridings, parties give the official nod to the candidates with status in the community, and those candidates usually happen to be male. In my experience, the grassroots members in any organization are more flexible about non-traditional candidates.

Call up the local party president and arrange an individual meeting with each member of the executive. They will be pleased that you have sought their help. Ask for their opinions before you decide to become a candidate. That way, they will feel they have a stake in the outcome of your decision. Once you have made up your mind, make sure that you involve existing members of the riding association. You need everyone's help in an election campaign, and while you understandably want to draw new people into the organization, you must not throw the baby out with the bathwater.

There is no magic to getting a nomination. The nod from on high, whether from the national party organization or the local executive group, is not essential. All support helps, and the more people you have on side, the easier it is. But the ultimate victory depends on organization. Too often, potential candidates think that they should not personally have to go out and seek members for the organization. They feel that once they have decided to run, the rest will fall into place. That is where an enterprising, hardworking newcomer has the edge. The nomination, like the election, is a numbers game; one extra supporter could mean the difference between winning and losing. So get your supporters out. They don't have to be longstanding members of any political organization. Many people get involved in politics for the first time because a friend has invited them out to a nomination fight. But they find that once they get involved, they have caught the bug and remain longstanding and loyal personal or party supporters.

Organization involves direct work from the candidate: calling, inviting, recruiting, encouraging. But the organization cannot win unless the candidate has a message.

That's why communications are so important. What have you brought into the political arena? Why are your running? Why would you be a good spokesperson for your community? You've got to believe in yourself. If you don't, nobody else will. If you understand why you're running and what your message is, you can better get the message out to the whole community. That involves direct communications with existing and prospective riding members. But it also involves indirect communication through the media.

Many would-be politicians flinch at the mere mention of the press. They conjure up visions of snarling hordes of reporters whose sole purpose in life is to make politicians miserable. That attitude dooms you to failure. You must be open, ready and willing to talk to the press. If you believe in yourself and your cause, and if you have a message, what better way is there? Remember: life isn't always easy for them either. Look at the general assignment reporters on the local newspapers. Many of them are required to master dozens of subjects in any given month. They don't always have the time to delve into the issues which you believe are of burning importance. So make their lives easier. Be open, be accessible and have ideas.

The local media are always looking for that special angle, the story which gives their newspaper, television or radio station the edge. If you can hand them the angle, chances are they will use it. A case in point: when I was preparing for the election of 1981, we knew for weeks that the election would be announced momentarily. The day before it was announced, I pounded out some press releases and distributed them as potential stories if the election were called. Included in the stories was a small filler about a long-standing Hamilton Liberal, Lela Daly, who had put a sign on her lawn for our party in every election for the past 60 years. I announced that when the election was called, I would be out there hammering in the sign. The result? The election was called the next day, and, out of more than 21 potential provincial candidates in the Hamilton area, I was the one with my picture on the front page, banging in the sign on the lawn of the veteran Liberal. Coincidence? Favoritism? No, I gave the local paper an interesting little story and they used it. There is nothing to stop any candidate from developing this kind of news sense.

Once you have established a good relationship with the press, they will come back to you. Don't be afraid of them. They have a job to do, and that job involves getting a message out to the people. They may err from time to time, but when they do, it's not in your best interest to jump down their throats. My motto throughout political life has always been, "Never complain, never explain." While, as with any rule, it has been broken, I find that in general it makes good sense not to complain about the press. When things are going badly, it's easy to blame them, but making them the scapegoats prevents us from confronting the real problem — our party or candidate strategy. When the provincial Liberal party was not doing well we would hear complaints every week in caucus about how bad the coverage was, and how we were going to go after that s.o.b. reporter who had written an uncomplimentary story. Oddly enough, when our luck turned — when we started to get positive press coverage for our initiatives — no one thought we should send thank-you notes to the press; we felt that the turnaround had been the result of our own efforts.

You will always run up against the odd reporter who has it out for you, who would criticize you for receiving the Nobel Peace Prize. But these are few and far between. Be open, be honest and be straightforward. The press will appreciate it because it will make their job easier. They may not always agree with you, but they'll know where you're coming from.

You now have the riding association on side and the press is willing to give you an even break. What next? If you are running in a provincial or federal election, you must first analyze the riding you want to represent. That means getting your hands on the results for the past three elections and breaking down the voting patterns in each poll. You will find pockets of strength or weakness for each party, and middle-ground areas known as the swing polls. Swing polls go from one party to the next depending on the issues of the day; you can literally watch the electorate move from one party to another, depending on national and regional trends.

As a general rule, the further away you are from the election, the more you concentrate on your weakest link. If a particular section of your riding is an absolute washout, spend some time well before the election trying to find out why. Does the area feel your party doesn't respond to its concerns? What are its special problems?

In my case, several years before the 1981 provincial election, I began working in an area that had consistently supported the New Democratic Party. The residents were skeptical of the two major parties and felt that no one really represented the interests of working people. In an effort to find out what their problems were, I organized an extensive door-to-door survey of 300 households, to identify the major concerns of the residents and their suggested solutions. One of their concerns was the perception at city hall that the neighbourhood had been taken over by transients who had no stake in the community. In fact, our survey was able to show that the average length of residence in this area was more than 30 years. We were obviously dealing with people who were deeply committed to their community.

The results of the survey were extremely useful in a local fight to save the neighbourhood school. We were able to prove that people *wanted* to live in the beach community and were not just in transit. The effect of the survey was twofold. It gave me a greater understanding of the community and its specific problems, and it gave the community a sense that I really cared. The survey had been carried out on weekends by myself and a team of volunteers, and quite clearly we were there because we wanted to learn about the community. In the past nobody had bothered to ask them what they really thought about their future. They appreciated our efforts. In the provincial election, we went from absolute annihilation in the area to a one-vote victory over the NDP. When the results from these polls came in on election night, there was a whoop of satisfaction from those who had been working for years to turn the area around. Our narrow victory proved that you could change the voting patterns of a community by listening and learning.

The second phase of the campaign involves swing areas. That means making yourself available to church picnics, to tea parties and to coffee klatches organized by party workers. The more people you have a chance to meet before the writ is issued, the greater are your chances of neutralizing the opposition. I say neutralizing because, notwithstanding party labels, in any election your repu- tation in the community is important. If people feel that you will be speaking out for their interests, if they are convinced that your primary concern is for the welfare of the community, then they will be prepared to throw aside party labels and vote for you.

A great number of Canadians comprise a massive group known as the switchers, those who vote for the person, rather than the party, or who may change party allegiance based on the issues of the day. The best chance you have to convince the switchers is by your own community involvement and by building their trust in the early stages of the election. Don't get too discouraged if the switchers don't come on board in droves. It's fair to say that in any federal election, the local candidate can only account for a 5 to 10 per cent differential in the vote. In other words, you are subject to national and regional trends. However, in a tight elec- tion a 5 per cent edge could mean the difference between winning and losing.

Your third objective is to concentrate your best efforts on your own and your party's supporters. Too often, novice politicians take their supporters for granted and spend all their time trying to woo the swing voters. Don't waste your time trying to win over your opponents. If you arrive as the Liberal candidate at someone's door and are told that the occupant has never voted Liberal in his life, don't waste your time trying to convince him. Just thank him politely and move on. The heat of the campaign is no time to win the opposition over to the Liberal cause. It may do wonders for your ego to spend half an hour talking about the greatness of your party, but meanwhile you have lost the chance to meet six other voters. The time to convince the doubters is in between elections.

When the election comes, don't tell the electors what the issues are; let them tell you. I remember watching a television show in which three federal candidates were being quizzed about the election issues. It was a major urban riding and the Liberal candidate said the most important issue was parking. I grimaced at the time, wondering why he would emphasize parking when we were facing major economic crises and issues of international proportions. But in retrospect, he was right. I don't know how many times I have knocked on doors and been told that the burning issue of the day was Mr. Kowalski's German shepherd or the potholes on Smith Street. The people will let you know what their problems are. It's your job to listen.

In my first election, I wanted to spend quality time with each voter. But when there are thousands of electors, you can't do this during a campaign. Election time tests your organization's skills; you must make sure every supporter, personal or party, is identified, and that every one of those supporters realizes how important it is to get to the polls.

This means that you must personally encourage and involve each and every campaign worker. Let them know how important their job is. Elections may be won or lost by a couple of votes in each poll. The job is never done until the last vote is counted. That means developing an organization which will make sure every last supporter gets to the polls.

During the last election, we faced an uphill battle, not only across the nation but in my own riding. Some party workers thought that I would win by a big margin, and even told prospective volunteers their services could be better used elsewhere. They forgot the basic rule in any election campaign: *Always run scared.* If that means starting your day at 6:00 am at the factory gates and working until midnight, so be it. The campaign period is the culmination of all your preparation and you can't afford to be overconfident or complacent. Always run scared, but don't panic.

Panic has a tendency to set in in the last days of a campaign which is floundering. Probably the best example was the Liberal campaign in the last federal election. We were going down, we *knew* we were going down, and yet we had to keep the workers searching for every morsel of support. The candidate feels the panic even more acutely than campaign workers. After all, you have the most to lose. When I ran federally, I had to resign my provincial seat; there was no looking back. Defeat meant the loss of my livelihood and the political life I loved so much. One way to avert panic is to focus on the job at hand. Your job as the candidate is to get out and meet the voters, to get your message across and to keep your troops buoyed.

It is absolutely critical that your team includes a campaign manager who has your trust and confidence. Delegate the whole job to your manager and let him or her run the show. Nothing is more counterproductive than a candidate who wants to personally direct every detail of his or her own campaign.

Your second most important appointment is your chief financial officer. Whatever the outcome, you do not want to emerge from the campaign with a heavy personal debt. You need someone who can exercise absolute control over all expenditures. Not a penny should go out of the political coffers — including petty cash — without the consent of your chief financial officer. That person may or may not help raise the money. And that brings us to the most problematic area in politics: fundraising.

Whenever I speak to a group of women who might be interested in running, one of the first questions they ask is about money. How much of your own money do you have to spend to be a candidate? Happily, with federal laws strictly limiting the amount that can be spent, the days when you could buy votes are gone. The laws covering expenses for federal campaigns guarantee a certain base of financial support if you win more than 15 per cent of the vote. Most provinces have also instituted laws to enforce spending limits and assist candidates financially. If you are considering running, money should never be a reason to say no.

In 1977, my personal contribution to my own campaign was $25. However, as a candidate, you will have to make other sacrifices which could be expensive. If you work, you may have to take an unpaid leave of absence. If you have children, you may have to pay for child care. Don't let financial considerations stop you from being a candidate. It's trite but true: Where there's a will, there's a way. I have never heard a candidate — winner or loser — express regret for having run. I've only heard regrets from those people who shied away from the chance to be a candidate.

Running in a campaign teaches you valuable things about yourself and your community. If you lose, you learn to lose gracefully. If you win, you realize it was a victory not for you, but for the dozens, or indeed hundreds, of people who worked on your behalf. Standing up for your ideas and ideals, facing your opponents head on in public debate, meeting the people at their doorsteps and responding to their concerns — all these will give you a greater understanding of yourself and the political process. And even if you lose money, those same people who helped in your campaign will help you wipe out the debt with fundraising dances, bake sales and other community ventures.

A special comment to mothers: the experience of motherhood is a particularly good preparation for politics. After all, supermum is expected to hold down a job, to to be chauffeur, negotiator, psychologist and nurse to her kids, to be a Jill of all trades and mistress of several. What better background for politics, where one is called on to digest an incredible array of information and take action based as much on gut instinct as on real answers?

You can do it, but only if you have the courage to try. You can probably think of 99 reasons to say no. But if you say yes, you have something to offer and your community will be the better for it.

Win, lose or draw, you have put your name on the line. You have shown that you are prepared to stand and be counted. You have disproved the naysayers and the doomsayers who never thought you had it in you.

Whatever happens, it's essential that you let your volunteers know how important they are. Throw a party, send handwritten thank-you notes, keep in touch by phone. These workers are the heart and soul of any organization, and without them even the star candidate is nothing. Any political machine is the sum of its parts, and the parts are people. They aren't there for individual gain but because they endorse you and your party's principles. They come out to help you again and again because they believe in you. One of the good things about being in opposition is that you really get a chance to separate the sheep from the goats. The people who put in token appearances on the campaign trail so that they could be first in line at the patronage trough have fled in droves. Most of them deserted before the election ended, because they could see the writing on the wall and wanted to ingratiate themselves with the ruling party.

A stint in opposition lets you find out who really supports the party for its principles and who is simply there for the free ride. The loyal workers, the ones who came out to work during a seemingly hopeless campaign, remain loyal and committed even in the depths of opposition. And a time in opposition allows you to reflect on what government is all about. You aren't there simply to grease the wheels of a bloated political machine. You're there to help all Canadians aspire to a certain level of equality.

So you've separated the wheat from the chaff; you know who your friends are, and you have thanked them. If you lose, what is your next step? If possible, decide whether you plan to run again. By making your views known, you can either keep your team together or allow time for a new candidate to emerge. When I lost the provincial election in 1977, I announced that night that I would be back. I had tasted politics and loved it. We can't always know when an election will be called, but the organizational work that goes into a winning campaign is never wasted.

Call your workers together at an early stage. Make them feel that they are important in planning for the next election. Keep every scrap of paper and every piece of information associated with the previous campaign. Lists of sign locations, lists of workers and identified supporters are invaluable in planning an inter-election strategy. Keep and update your information on community groups and special interest groups. Specialized directories (e.g. of ethnic groups or community organizations) can be an excellent source of contact in urban areas. Information about ratepayers and recreational organizations is helpful.

Assimilate all your information and bring together as many people as possible to plan your next step. Take heart; an election loss is not always a blueprint for political oblivion. Political war-horses have run several times before being elected. Winning depends on a number of factors, including not only the organization, the candidate and the party message, but also a large dollop of luck and being in the right place at the right time. Any of these can work against you in the first election, or even in the second.

It's up to you to maximize all the positive factors within your control so that outside forces, including national and regional trends, cannot keep you from ultimate victory. The best time to do this is in between elections.

The inter-election period is when you can reach out to the community, taking every possible opportunity to meet people at large and small gatherings. Divide your riding into about a dozen areas. Assign each area to one of your more committed workers, preferably one who lives in the neighbourhood. He or she will be your eyes and ears in that neighbourhood. Is a tricky zoning question coming up on city council? You should be there. Even when the issue rightfully belongs in another jurisdiction, you should be involved. Most voters aren't concerned with electoral boundaries.

They do understand when a candidate cares enough about the community to get involved in an issue that affects their neighbourhood. Speak out on their behalf, and arrange to meet in small groups. Block each area off into a dozen smaller units, again with a unit captain in each area to keep you informed. Use flyers to invite people to an informal evening of coffee, cookies and politics. Most people won't even show up. But the fact that you have taken the time *in between elections* to ask their advice and opinions is a plus. Those who come may not want to talk about politics; they might be more interested in what kind of person you are or how you can help them with a parking problem.

If you decide not to run again, the time you have invested in your community will not be wasted. You will have made friends with people whom you might otherwise never have met. Some of these friendships last a lifetime. I know of no other profession where you can meet so many people with such diverse backgrounds all bound together by one compelling interest, their love of politics. I have met bus drivers and bank presidents, doctors and ditch-diggers. I have made friendships that will remain with me long after I leave politics. And I have come to know my own community in a way that otherwise never would have been possible. I have visited the open hearths of the steel mills; I've seen the innards of a shoe factory and a textile mill. And I've caught a glimpse of the struggle of ordinary people who face the extraordinary challenge of making ends meet. I can honestly say that, win, lose or draw, your communion with the community will make it all worthwhile.

15

Communion with Community

Rule 15: Know where you come from to know where you're going

Hamilton is a steel town. The city's name evokes visions of the Tiger Cats' football team and sputtering smokestacks. The popular image isn't pretty — a grim, industrial skyline of smokestacks pitted against a grey, hazy sky.

"So you're from Hamilton," they say, sniggering slightly. The implication is that someone would rather be from Mars than from Canada's godforsaken industrial heartland. But they don't know Hamilton like I do. They don't know it as a city of working people, of labourers and immigrants who came here to make a better life for their children.

They could be Cape Bretoners, like my maternal grandfather who came to Hamilton in 1924. Their homeland could be Italy; thousands of Italian-speaking labourers arrived in Hamilton in the post-war years. They could be among the new wave of Chinese and Vietnamese who fled the traumatic civil wars in their native countries. Whatever their background, they have come to Hamilton seeking a new chance.

My father came from Timmins. He was working for a small radio station in northern Ontario back in the mid-1940s when he received a job offer in Hamilton. My father didn't know the city. But the offer came from Tommy Darling, a transplanted northern broadcaster, and my father did know Tommy Darling. He pulled up stakes and moved to the big city.

Like many new Hamiltonians, my father quickly discovered the city's warmth and became a major booster. He worked as a sports announcer and advertising salesman at a major local radio station. My mother, a native Hamiltonian, actually met my father through his work in sports. She worked as a secretary at the Steel Company of Canada and was active in the industrial ladies' softball league. She was in charge of publicity, and that meant getting the scores to my father in the hopes he might broadcast them. My father asked her out. She really didn't want to go, but was afraid that if she didn't, he wouldn't air the team scores. So blossomed a sports romance that would eventually span four decades.

My parents were married in late November 1948, and the wedding had to be postponed in case our Tiger Cats made it to the finals. In future years, whenever my mother complained about the long hours and the sacrifices involved in politics, I reminded her that she must have known what she was getting into when her wedding was postponed for sports. Sports, politics and Hamilton were intertwined throughout my youth. The Tiger Cats had put us on the map with their colourful front line. We thrilled to names like Angela Mosca and John Barrow. As youngsters, Hamiltonians first learned the distinctive Tigers' cheer of *Oskee wee wee. Oskee wa wa Holy mackinaw tigers, eat em raw.*

At one point, the city even owned the team, and in my father's first election campaign in 1960, one of the issues was whether or not we should sell. My father was vehemently opposed. Even though the team was losing money, he felt we could not buy the kind of civic pride and fame that went along with the Tiger Cats. He ran for controller and part of his platform was to keep the team. He was elected, but the team was sold. One of the new owners' first acts was to fire him from a job he had held for more than a decade.

He was philosophical about the job loss; he would rather fight for his principles and lose than give in for the sake of a job.

My father always took the view that what was best for Hamilton was right. I still remember the fight he put up to encourage the Canadian Football Hall of Fame to settle in Hamilton. Because Hamilton is so close to Toronto, we have always tended to live in its shadow and lose out as the centre for any major attraction. My dad fought to change that. He believed that the Football Hall of Fame rightfully belonged in the city that breathed, lived and loved the game. He was so convinced that when a group of private backers for the project reneged, he mortgaged our home to ensure the interim financing as required by the Canadian Football League. My mother had to co-sign the mortgage, and my father realized that she might not be quite as deeply committed to the Hall of Fame project as he was. He told her he had some papers at the bank for her to sign and went with her so that she wouldn't raise hell in front of the bank manager when she realized that they were putting their house on the line. The deed was done; my mother had no choice but to give in, but the fireworks flew later. It never occurred to my father that we might have to sacrifice our house as result of his committed exuberance. He was such a believer in the power of positive thinking that he never entertained any thought of failure.

When he was first elected mayor in 1962, he gave an interview to the Toronto *Globe and Mail* about his vision for the city. It included a totally revitalized downtown core with theatres, shops and hotels. He began to plan a major theatre complex, along with a convention centre, art gallery and hockey arena. Properties were expropriated and political mayhem followed. It was hard to visualize a dream when bustling businesses were replaced by vacant lots during the time it took for all the pieces to come together.

The theatre came first. It gave Hamiltonians a chance to prove that we are a city with heart. Instead of depending on funding by the provincial and federal governments, my father and a group of

139

community leaders embarked on a campaign to show that we could support our own theatre. Almost every night, my dad conducted tours through the half-built theatre, convincing individuals and groups to contribute to the community by buying a seat.

The mayor as chief salesman, you might laugh. In reality any mayor is a salesman for his or her city. He or she must convince investors that Hamilton or Ottawa or Halifax is a great place to be, that we are our own biggest backers. As the years went on, my father's work progressed. The jewel in the crown was to be a major NHL-sized arena which would keep Hamilton in the fore-front of professional sports across the country. He had lined up a group of private investors who were prepared to build the arena themselves if the city would rent ice time. He fought, he lobbied, he *lived* the arena proposal. But it was turned down in what he considered to be one of his worst defeats at city hall.

Shortly afterwards my father suffered a heart attack which effectively removed him from public life. As with many former jocks who see middle age staring them in the face, he had taken up jogging. As usual, he went at it tooth and nail. He wasn't going to run around the block; he intended to successfully complete the Boston Marathon. Maybe the fact that Boston had a fellow Irish mayor had something to do with it. To prepare for the Boston run, he entered North America's oldest marathon, Hamilton's Around the Bay Road Race. In 1975 he had run seven miles of the race and then dropped out. In 1976, he was convinced he would go all the way. So at age 57, he started out on a marathon that would drastically change his life.

He was bringing up the rear when he collapsed and his heart stopped beating. He was immediately revived and rushed to hospital, but on the way there his heart stopped again. On arrival, it was estimated that he had been without oxygen for a total of ten minutes. He sank into a deep coma and the doctors prepared us for the worst. It was unlikely he could ever survive such a blow to his system. We were devastated. But we rallied around in the belief

140

that where there is life, there is hope. Friends and relatives gathered to say the rosary in the presence of my unconscious father. He remained in a coma for three weeks, then was semi-conscious for another three weeks. As he started to come to the surface he could neither speak nor move. He was completely paralysed and the sounds he made came out as a stream of nonsense — what the medical profession calls a 'word salad'.

Following his return to consciousness, he was transfered to a rehabilitation hospital which was known for its work with stroke victims. Because his heart attack had deprived his brain of oxygen, his symptoms were similar to those suffered by stroke patients. He had to learn to walk again and couldn't remember how to read or write. His physical recovery far outstripped the predictions of the medical profession, but the brain damage was permanent; to this day, he remains confused and dependent, unable to properly express himself or even to totally comprehend his condition. It's as though he is on the verge of understanding, on the verge of consciousness, but never quite makes it. He knows his brain is damaged, and he lives in the present. But he doesn't totally comprehend the degree of his difficulty. He can't feed or care for himself, and my mother has to care for him as if he were a small child. It has been hard for her, and for us.

During his crisis, it was his family that stood by him. Although my father's illness had happened while he was still in office, it became clear that his political allies and acquaintances weren't prepared to give him the same support. During his early days in the hospital, his old buddies from the Knights of Columbus and various political friends would come out and wish him well. But when it became obvious that he would never fully recover, that he could never be mayor again, the visits became fewer and fewer. It was as though Vic Copps had dropped off the face of the earth and all those who had valued him as mayor had written him off for dead.

They didn't see him as I saw him. Even in the face of incredible

141

odds, he fought for his life with dignity. His spirit could not be quelled. One day he was pacing up and down the corridor of the hospital. He was confused, and didn't really know where he was, but he had to keep moving. I asked him where he was going in such a hurry. "I have to move to live," he said. And when he would cry out, in language that bared an untold frustration, I could only say, "Thank God that you still have the spirit to cry out." His old friends would say they couldn't visit him because, "I can't bear seeing your father this way. I would rather remember him as he was." What they don't realize is that a person who spends ten years of his or her life as an invalid is still alive and needs the stimulation the outside world can bring. What they refuse to realize is that by facing up to illness, they can better understand their own mortality and come to some realization of why we are here in the first place.

We are here, we get involved, we work for our community, not only because we gain a certain amount of satisfaction from making our mark, but also to make a better life for our families and for those around us. Politics is a means to improve the quality of life. But the moment politics interferes with my ability to do the best for my family is the moment I get out. I've seen what my father went through. I love politics but I am also a realist. Up one day, down the next. At the centre of things one year, out in the cold the next. If you don't have a personal sense of mission and a supportive family, all the plaudits in the world are not going to make politics worthwhile. Keep it in perspective; you do your best but there are no guarantees.

When I look to my own father, I can honestly say that notwithstanding his disability, he lives each day to the fullest. He loved his city and he loved his job. If he had to do it all over again, he wouldn't change. Most of us would hope to be able to say that about our own lives.

The other heartening thing was the response of ordinary people in the community. Not a day goes by in Hamilton that someone doesn't ask about my father. Ten years later, they remember a small kindness or a special hello.

At the time of his illness, my father was in a difficult financial position. He didn't have a large pension, since local politicians had only been included in the municipal pension plan about four years before his illness. A group of concerned community members, headed by John Munro, organized a 'Thanks Vic' day. It was intended not only to raise money for my father but also to allow Hamilton's ordinary citizens to thank him. They organized a $100 plate dinner which saw both hotels filled to capacity. They sold 'Thanks Vic' buttons for a dollar each at a Tiger Cats' game. They raised a whopping $170,000 trust fund in my father's name. The interest supports him now and, after his death, the principal will be turned over to a Hamilton performing arts trust, which is just the way he would have wanted it. From the community and back to the community.

Meanwhile, my mother, Geraldine, began to pick up the pieces of her life. She had not held a permanent job outside the home since her marriage, but she was thrust back into the job market. Again thanks to John Munro (the only politician who ever took the time to visit my father) my mother was appointed a citizenship judge. When the position was offered, she was scared stiff. But with no other financial lifeline, she didn't have a choice. Within two months of my father's heart attack, my mother was working full-time for the first time in more than 25 years.

They say it's an ill wind that blows no good. While my father's increasing dependency took its toll on the family in some respects, it allowed my mother to blossom in a way she had never dreamed possible. Her new job involved public speaking and travelling the whole of the Niagara horseshoe as a citizenship judge. She juggled the full-time job with her home responsibilities, having decided that she would not follow the social worker's advice to put my father into a nursing home.

For almost ten years, she kept up both ends of her job, helping my father at home and working full-time. Her appointment expired in February of 1985, a few months after the Tories arrived in office. It was not renewed. Although my mother had been appointed by the Liberal government, she had distinguished herself by remaining totally above partisan politics and doing her job in a way that brought praise from all sides. Her ability, and my father's reputation, prompted the regional council to pass a unanimous resolution calling on the prime minister to reinstate my mother in her job. The resolution was approved by members of all political parties, and local members of Parliament from the New Democratic and Conservative parties spoke out publicly on her behalf. But it did no good.

At first she received verbal notice that her appointment would not be renewed. When that news became public, all hell broke loose in Hamilton. There was a flood of support from members of all political parties and the minister responsible said that no decision had been made. The issue dragged on for weeks. No one was willing either to fire my mother or reinstate her. Finally the Kitchener-Waterloo *Record* got the story. The minister responsible, Walter McLean, revealed the government's position. He said that my mother's appointment had not been renewed in part because her daughter had been vocal in her opposition to the government. I was outraged. Never had the sins of the daughter been visited so visibly on the mother. I rose in the House of Commons on a question of privilege. Does that mean that every relative of an opposition member of Parliament has to face reprisals, even to losing his or her job?

As it turned out the decision was made, not by McLean, but by a political group headed by then deputy prime minister, Erik Niel-sen. I had been told confidentially by a Conservative MP who knew my mother well, that her appointment had been passed by the regional group of Conservative members which examines such appointments. It wasn't until final approval came to a select com-mittee including the deputy prime minister that my mother was turfed out. According to cabinet tradition, McLean, as the minister responsible, had to defend the decision publicly although it was clear that if it had been up to him, my mother would have kept her job.

The issue, I am sure, was small potatoes to Conservatives who had waited so long to get their share of the action. As the prime minister often said, "You dance with them that brung you." It didn't matter that my mother danced with no one and that her job and her care for my father had consumed all her energy for the past decade; that she was so scrupulous about staying out of politics that she wouldn't even go to my headquarters the night of my September 4th victory. She was remotely associated with the former Liberal administration and that was enough to secure her dismissal.

Again the community rallied round. My mother decided that if she couldn't beat them, she might as well join them. A political novice, she ran in the local elections as alderman in the ward where she had lived all her life. She topped the polls, unseating two veterans. At age 60 she launched a third career. The night of the election, when asked by the local newspaper how she felt about her victory, she said, "It is the best thing that ever happened in my life."

Like many women, she had worked in the past for her husband and for each of her children. This was the first time she had undergone the same effort for her own career. Like many women she understood her community, but was afraid to stand as a can-didate. At the press conference to announce her candidacy, she started off in a shaky voice and appeared quite nervous. However, as she got warmed up, it became easier and easier. Now, after several months on the job as alderman for ward four, she is becoming an old pro.

So never say you're too old. If you think it can't be done, just take a chance and go for it. My mother did, and it paid off in spades.

16

The Core of the Matter

Rule 16: Your community always comes first

As a Liberal, I have a pragmatic approach to life. I am not tied to a doctrine which may or may not respond well to the problems of the day. Unlike the Conservatives, I do not believe the private sector can always do it better. In the areas of health care, education and social services, it can be argued that the public sector does do it better. Conversely, Liberals are not wedded to the NDP's socialist approach. Pragmatism doesn't mean expediency. Individual liberty must be paramount, but never at the expense of the common good. These centrist themes must certainly dominate the long-term agenda of our party and our country. At the same time, as an ordinary MP, I like to be able to see the fruits of my labour. I like to know that my work is productive and that I am more than a voice in the wilderness. How to do this? By reaching out to the community, trying to help those who cannot help themselves. And this means constituency work.

This is no easy job. Besides your responsibilities in the House and in committee, you must keep up to date on hundreds of enquiries which flood your office weekly on subjects from animal rights to university research funding. People write to you to complain that Air Canada ruined their vacation plans or that a court case is causing problems. Some letters are straightforward; others include detailed analyses which must be carefully studied before you can respond.

You are also called on to help individuals in your own riding. Some are unemployed and want to cut through the red tape to receive their UI benefits; but more often, they need help to develop the skills to find a job. Someone who has been with the same company for 20 years may not even understand the strategies involved in looking for a job. Other constituents need help in immigration cases or want to take advantage of government assistance programmes for small businesses. Whatever the question, they contact their member of Parliament and they want action.

I usually try to meet personally with constituents in my riding office once a week. That gives them a chance to explain their difficulties in person, and it also helps me keep in touch with what's going on in the community. Ottawa is a sort of Disneyland North; only by returning to the riding on a regular basis can I keep in touch with the needs and aspirations of my fellow citizens.

When I visit the riding office each week and speak to individuals about their own problems or their concerns for their children, I realize this is the stuff of government. An injured worker has spent all his life as a construction labourer; at 50, he is laid off because of back problems. The Workers Compensation Board says he is suffering from degenerative disc disease and that his problem has nothing to do with his employment (30 years of pick-and-shovel work). Degenerative disc disease disqualifies him from workers' compensation. He may have a small pension, but more likely he will be forced to apply for welfare. His wife has never worked and her chances of finding a job are virtually nil. He feels castrated, unable to provide for his family, and spends most of his days moping around the house. He begins to drink too much. His wife is in a state of emotional exhaustion. The couple sticks together, but their life has begun to fall apart.

Does it sound like something out of a soap opera? Unfortunately, this kind of scenario unfolds across the country, wherever ordinary men and women are plagued by unemployment, poor health or a failing economy. Politicians can offer sympathy, and in some cases they may be able to break through the red tape. But all too often, our hands are tied.

Immigration decisions are often just as distressing. A large proportion of my constituency work involves applications by families to be reunited. If an adult child lives in another country, his chances of joining parents, brothers or sisters in Canada are minimal unless he has specific skills which are unavailable in our country. Imagine the frustration of a mother who fled her native land with her husband and left behind a six-year-old daughter, since it was the family's only chance of ever living a free life. The daughter is being cared for by grandparents while the parents' application for political refugee status is being processed. The child will be allowed to join her parents when they have permanent status in Canada. The couple has waited eighteen months, and they still don't even have an appointment for their hearing. The mother breaks down crying in my office as she shows me her child's most recent photograph.

This kind of frustration and heartbreak faces most members of Parliament every time they visit their constituency offices. I can tell you, a day in my riding office is ten times more draining, physically and emotionally, than a week of speeches in the House of Commons. To debate is easy; to confront real problems and know there are no easy solutions is frightening. In some cases there are solutions, as in the issue of immigration. It would certainly be possible for the government to relax the rules regarding family reunification to permit the influx of greater numbers of immigrants into our country. But for every action there is a reaction. It has never been proven that immigrants take jobs away from Canadians, but when economic times are difficult government has always reduced immigration. Could the current pressure to close the door have something to do with the fact that so many recent newcomers are non-white? We like to see ourselves as non-racist, but are we?

Look at today's lost generation. Young people often leave school with few marketable skills and little understanding of even how to look for a job. Without experience, even those who do have marketable skills are caught in a Catch–22 situation. No experience, no job: no job, no experience. The result is an unendurable unemployment rate in the nineteen- to 25-year-old age group. No politician has the answers. These kids have begun to feel that society has forgotten them.

When I graduated from university I sent out four job applications. One newspaper offered me summer employment and subsequently hired me full-time. The possibility of any graduate now getting a job after four applications is almost nonexistent. What answers can a politician provide to a frustrated 20-year-old who waves sheets of job rejections, despairing of ever finding work? What hope is there for a seventeen-year-old who hasn't the slightest idea what a resumé is? You can offer suggestions, direction and encouragement, but the economic climate which governs the job market is largely beyond your control. Your frustrations, therefore, are almost as great as theirs. So many need help, and there's so little help you can give them.

The greatest danger you confront is becoming callous. It's so much easier to believe that anybody who can't find a job doesn't really want one; that anyone on workers compensation is faking it. It's easier to talk about welfare bums than it is to confront real poverty. The horror stories in the constituency are very real indeed. Of course there are some fakers and bums. But when 20 per cent of the local population is unemployed, you can't talk about milking the system.

It isn't enough just to be available in the riding office. People want to feel that you are a continuing part of the community. So Friday and Saturday nights are reserved for 'making the rounds', attending social events and dances, taking time out from politics to stay in touch. On any given Saturday night, I could be attending an Italian dance, a Portuguese gathering or a Pakistani community celebration. Sunday might mean a special church service or remembrance ceremony. There's always something on in the community.

As a member, you have a special responsibility to the party organizations in your riding and community. Good political organizations don't sleep between elections. They continue to involve people, to build their membership and to make sure the party is visible. That means regular meetings to plan conferences and social functions, and open houses and coffee parties to nurture growth in the organization. Between elections, some people will move on and others will join the party. If you allow your local organization to lie dormant, you may find only the skeleton of a team once the next election rolls around.

Social functions do more than allow party supporters to socialize and meet their members of Parliament. They are also financially essential. If dances and boat rides let people get together, they also allow the local party organization to fill its coffers between elections. Any healthy riding organization needs a couple of fundraising events a year to build up a war chest for the next election, and to ensure that it has the funds to carry on the ordinary business of keeping in touch with its members.

Most political parties have local and regional organizations. When the leader comes to town, a number of ridings will cooperate to put together a good crowd at a fundraising dinner and to divide logistical responsibilities. Local organizations may get even more ambitious. In 1986, for the first time in the history of the federal Liberal party, the Ontario convention was moved from Toronto to Hamilton. This happened when, in 1985, a group of interested Liberals and Hamiltonians persuaded the annual convention that all communities across Ontario should be allowed to host a Liberal convention. The job of convincing the 1985 delegates was not easy and the change required a constitutional amendment. The previous constitution allowed the party executive to choose the location for the convention and inevitably the choice was Toronto. The amendment permitted the delegates themselves to vote on the location of the next year's convention. The Hamilton group pulled out all the stops to make sure our city would be the choice for 1986. We even convinced the mayor of Hamilton, a Conservative, to travel to Toronto to host a reception to convince the Liberal delegates that we really wanted them in our city.

Planning and preparation for the convention began a year in advance. Several months before the actual event, the committee began meeting weekly in preparation for the largest political convention (other than a leadership convention) ever held in the province of Ontario. The whole community got involved and the convention was a roaring success. It gave not only local Liberals but all of Hamilton a lift. Business boomed, and the local newspaper printed a glowing editorial. The Liberal convention proved what a fine convention city we had. The effort involved the whole community. The convention committee was co-chaired by a local alderman, Shirley Collins, and lawyer Milt Lewis. Several hundred volunteers were involved in everything from ensuring security to directing the out-of-towners to area tourist attractions. I've rarely been so proud of my home town.

Does this all seem rather prosaic? Even a little boring? It isn't, let me tell you. Certainly it's a long way from a beerfest at a German community celebration to the sonorous halls of Parliament. Inevitably there are those who prefer the smoke and mirrors of national politics to the sheer slogging involved in constituency and community work. But I'm not one of them.

Without Hamilton, I'd be nothing at all. It's not only because my riding elected me — I work very hard to earn my constituents' trust and respect, to say nothing of their votes. Yes, I do have to stay on their good side if I want to continue to be their member of Parliament. But that's not why I do it.

Partly, I get a real charge out of doing what I can. If the frustrations are great, so are the rewards when something does work out, when I can really help someone. And partly, constituency work is my way of keeping my feet on the ground. It's too easy, in Ottawa, to forget what the rest of the country is like. And that's a recipe not only for political disaster, but also for a sort of insanity. Once you lose touch with your community, you go a little flippy; I've seen it happen.

But mostly, I do the work and spend the time because I love Hamilton. It's my home, my history, part of my core. Some Maritimers have a phrase for it; they ask a stranger not "Where do you come from?" but "Where do you belong to?" There's a big difference between coming from and belonging to, and Hamilton is where I belong. I don't care what my constituency work costs me in time, work or energy. My community deserves everything I can bring to it. And then some.

CHAPTER

17

Paradise Lost

Rule 17: (Rao's law) The only way out of this mess is through it

The first time I met John Turner was when he was *not* running for office. He was working in Toronto for the prestigious law firm of McMillan, Binch, and waiting on the sidelines while the Liberal government in Ottawa was fighting a worldwide recession. I got a call from a mutual friend, Gordon Ryan, a Toronto stockbroker. Gord had been a member of the original Turner 195 club (those delegates who voted for Turner even on the last ballot at the 1968 Liberal leadership convention). He was also one of my advisors when I ran for the provincial leadership. Gord said that someone would like to have lunch with me. "Sure," I said, "Sounds great, who?" "John Turner," he said. I laughed; why would John Turner want to have lunch with me? There was no leadership race in the offing, and I wondered why he should want to meet me now. But I was intrigued by the chance to meet the man who had been touted as the next Liberal leader and prime minister.

We were to meet on Friday afternoon in the Imperial Room at the Royal York. I wanted to keep the meeting discreet since I didn't want to be visibly aligned with any leadership candidate, real or potential. I was late. John swept up to meet me and ushered me over to a table on a small dais which had a commanding view of the elegant sweep of the room. The first thing that struck me about him was the flash of his penetrating blue eyes. When he spoke, the intensity of his look could be at once flattering and frightening. The lunch was leisurely. I had a chance to learn of his background in politics and his concern for the future of the party. He spoke about the difficult organizational problems we faced and the concern over our mounting debt. I didn't agree or disagree, I merely absorbed. I knew perfectly well that the meeting was a little more than a social call.

At the end of the lunch, my hopes for discretion were dashed when Keith Davey jumped out from behind a potted palm, less than eight feet away. Keith just happened to be having lunch with Senator Ian Sinclair. Keith hadn't acknowledged our presence until the end of the meal, and I wondered how much he had heard and what he thought. His hello to John was at best perfunctory. It was obvious that he was unlikely to support Turner's bid for the leadership.

After lunch Turner invited me back to his office. The inner sanctum revealed the two loves of his life, his family and politics. Family photographs showing the human side of John and Geills were interspersed with photos of some of his favorite political heroes, people like Bobby Kennedy and Lester Pearson. It was clear that, although John was several hundred kilometres from Ottawa, he was still in love with politics.

I must admit, my first reaction was not positive. I had already made up my mind that I was not to be converted by Old Blue Eyes — a man who had left the ranks in the mid-1970s and sat on the sidelines while the party was going through a turbulent period. Although he seemed more human than I had expected, I was determined not to support him.

The man I met was eager to make friends and curiously shy. He projected the warmth of a father and the remoteness of a born winner. His ambivalence was almost endearing, a quality which was never apparent in the press releases about the brilliant young man who had challenged Trudeau for the leadership in 1968. It wasn't until after John Turner's election to the leadership of our party that I was again able to have so intimate a glimpse of the man.

The second time I met John Turner, he was in the throes of the most difficult challenge of his life, the 1984 election. In a last-ditch attempt to woo the women's vote — women had traditionally voted Liberal — Turner had called all the women candidates to meet in Ottawa to discuss issues affecting women. You can image the dynamics of a meeting involving about 40 women candidates and the leader, in the middle of a campaign which had been less than successful. It was at that meeting that I met future Liberal members Lucie Pépin and Sheila Finestone for the first time. It was a dynamic and impressive group. We let loose at the in-camera session on a variety of issues, including bum-patting. It was a verbal slugfest, no holds barred, and it didn't always flatter our leader. In a manner which I now realize is typical of his approach, John absorbed the suggestions and the criticisms without becoming defensive. He genuinely wanted our opinions and was sincere about listening to our beefs.

Following the meeting he appeared at a press conference, flanked by July Erola and several dozen women candidates. Although most journalists were more interested in bum-patting than in equal pay, one particularly well-informed reporter began to go after him on the party's commitment to equal value legislation. After all, the Liberals had been in power for the past two decades and what had we done to help women in this country? As the questioner probed, it became clear that our leader really wasn't sure government policies could be used to implement equal value legislation. At this point Judy Erola stepped in authoritatively to settle the reporter's doubts. But the message wasn't lost on anyone: John Turner really did not understand the question of equality through government legislation, and what's more, he was prepared to admit it. Unlike most politicians, when he didn't have the answer to a question, he wasn't prepared to fake it. He was only prepared to tell the truth as he saw it. That honesty was apparent again in his famous response to the patronage question. "Why did you accept Trudeau's appointments?" Mulroney asked. Turner said simply, "I had no option" and, for his candour, was pilloried coast to coast by his opponent.

In the short term, there is no doubt that political naiveté cost John Turner and cost him dearly. But in the long term, his commitment to the truth may be his strongest asset — especially against the current prime minister.

It's easy to be graceful and magnanimous when you're on top, but when you're going down, the claws come out. What I saw in John Turner, during the worst days of the campaign when it seemed nothing would go right, was that he wasn't prepared to claw. He wasn't interested in taking out anything or anybody who stood in his way. He believed in the old verities: fight a good fight and take your lumps like a soldier. This sense of responsibility came out so clearly in his concession speech on the night of the election, when he said that the people had spoken and the people were always right. Whatever he thought of the outcome, he was no whiner. He respected the process so much that he never complained about the choice of the people.

The defeat itself was a humbling experience for a man who had spent his whole life winning. He was a social winner; before marrying Geills he had even been touted as an escort to Princess Margaret. He was a winner in school, as a Rhodes scholar and law student. Whatever he put his hand to, he seemed to turn into success. He was a winner in politics, the only member of Parliament ever to be elected from three different provinces. He was even a winner in the eyes of the media and the Liberal party, a party which had pinned its hopes for survival on the blue-eyed boy from Bay Street.

After a lifetime of winning, he was forced very publicly to face the ignominy of defeat. No longer was his table at Winston's the coveted one. 'His' salad would probably be replaced by Mulroney baloney. But he fully respected the people's right to throw him out; he fundamentally believed that the people were always right.

It's easier to judge someone in defeat than in victory. In defeat, Turner was generous and uncomplaining, upholding the principles of democracy and trying to rebuild a flagging and motley party. For those who had supported him because they thought he was a winner, he had to begin the leadership race all over again. He had to keep his sights set on the long-term possibilities. And he had to convince us that he was the person to do the job because, in defeat, he had learned victory.

He had shown that he would not run away; he would face the music. He faced it that night in Vancouver Quadra. When the country fell about him, he kept his grace.

He did not run away because his motivation had not been solely power. He wanted to build a new Liberal party with modern approaches to today's problems, and he seized the opportunity to rebuild from ground zero.

I didn't know John Turner very well when I joined his team. But I can honestly say that he has listened and learned from the process in a way unique among politicians. I can vouch for his involvement.

Most of us think we already have all the answers. We'd rather lecture than listen. Not so with John Turner. At caucus meetings, he listens intently, jotting down notes so that he can respond to each question or concern. Within the party, he has shown a willingness not only to get up and give speeches, but to participate in workshops, to listen to the grassroots. One could be cynical and say that this listening goes hand in hand with being in opposition.

Heaven knows, the exigencies of government sometimes separate the politicians from the real party people. But with John Turner, you get the sense that he is genuinely listening, not ego stroking or giving lip service. He wants our party to reflect the concerns of each ordinary member.

On a personal note, I have found him to be sincere and approachable. The first time he met my husband was at a party in Toronto thrown by financial mogul Hal Jackman. The guest list read like a veritable who's who of Canadian business. Ric was visiting from Florida. For all John knew, he might never see him again. Unlike many politicians on the cocktail circuit, who talk to you until someone more important comes along, John went out of his way to make sure Ric felt at home.

It is that feeling of sincerity and honest friendship which distinguishes him from many politicians. When he came to Hamilton for the Liberal convention, he asked whether he could have a private visit with my ailing father. Although I advised him against it, I appreciated the thought. On Sunday morning, we met for mass at St. Patrick's Catholic Church. Unannounced, Turner slipped into a side pew because he didn't want anyone to make a fuss over his attendance. The little things, untrumpeted but not unnoticed by party members, are among the reasons he has managed to build a solid base of support.

He's come a long way from Vancouver Quadra and he's still going strong.

18

You've Come A Long Way, Baby

Rule 18: If it gobbles when it talks, it's a turkey

Working on the Hill is like being drowned in a sea of pin-striped suits. Oh, there are plenty of women around, but most of them are taking dictation, recording Hansard or fetching coffee. When the mainly male ministers come into committee, they bring teams of bright young men prepared to face the opposition's onslaught over the estimated annual budget. The YUMMIES (Young Urban Men) are in evidence everywhere.

If a young man wants to have a solid career, what better starting place is there than with a minister on the Hill? Along with the young turks, motivated by their desire for a return to fiscal conservatism (dog eat pup) there are the senior male mandarins, most of whom have worked their way up the ladder through the traditional networks.

It could be argued that women haven't been in the public service long enough to warrant senior management positions. But when you look at the incredible progress in the area of bilingual and francophone senior staff over the past two decades, you realize that what is missing is the political will to improve the status of women. It's not only the bureaucracy which lacks political will. Many

After the deed was done, July 6, 1985.

An unusual trio. Pierre Trudeau, John Turner (in foreground) and Jean Chrétien dine together at the 80th birthday of Jack Pickersgill, one of the "four horsemen" who led the Liberals back to power following the Diefenbaker era. (November 1985)

I'm not the only Copps with a big mouth. Sisters Mary (left) and Brenda help celebrate election night. (September, 1984)

Photo by Rodney C. Daw

A proud moment. My provincial colleagues salute unanimous passage of my Pay Equity Bill.

With David Peterson and now cabinet Minister Lily Munro, to launch the by-election after my Hamilton Centre resignation.

With Liberal party president, Iona Campagnolo, at a fundraising dinner for John Munro.

Photo by Carmen Rizzotto

Touring Hamilton's waste recycling plant with Environment Minister Charles Caccia.

On the hustings in a Hamilton factory.

Meeting the workers at local plant gates—at 6 a.m.!

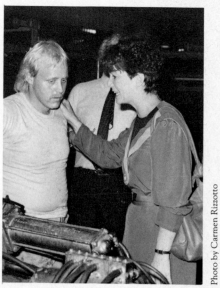

Photo by Carmen Rizzotto

On assignment as a cub reporter for the Hamilton Spectator.

On the job injury. While covering the Canusa basketball games as a reporter, I got into the act and was promptly stepped on. No, I didn't climb over any chairs.

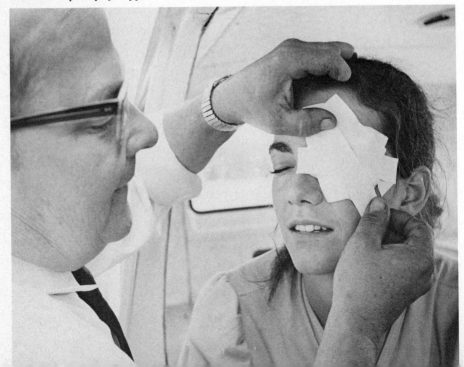

Here I am at age 2, already trying to tame a tiger.

A family photo at Canada's largest annual Christmas party at Dofasco in 1965. From left Brenda, my father, me, Mary, my mother, Kevin.

That's me on the right, fighting for my sister in her successful campaign as president of the Catholic Youth Organization Crusader Club. From left, Brenda, and winner, Mary. (1962)

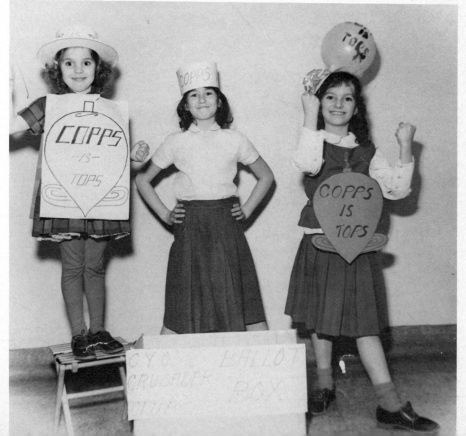

At a Bob Kaplan fundraiser with fellow Rat Packers Don Boudria (left) and John Nunziata.

Some of the soul behind my work. From left, intern Shelley Gilmour, staffers Barry Strader, Danielle May and Gordon Douglas.

A daily vigil with Jacques Hébert helped keep spirits up during the hunger strike. John Nunziata joins us here.

A scrum with John Nunziata following the Sinclair Stevens resignation.

members of Parliament, including ministers, really believe that a woman's place is in the home, not the House.

John Crosbie is a case in point. The minister formerly responsible for the implementation of equality recommendations and for dealing with the Charter of Rights can't seem to keep his own sexist opinions under control. That all came to light in the House of Commons one day. Mr. Crosbie was under attack for having awarded a job to his son. He was screaming and yelling, calling Bob Kaplan every name in the book, when I heckled, "Is there a doctor in the House?" His retort was, "Just quieten down, baby. You bunch of poltroons can shout all you like. The Rat Pack can quieten down. The titmice can quieten down."

I rose in my place and stated very emphatically, "I am 32 years old, I am an elected member of Parliament from Hamilton East and I'm nobody's baby." I asked the minister to apologize. He did not. Dissatisfied, I decided to confront him outside the House and ask for his apology. He was holding an impromptu press conference to explain his son's new job. Just as the conference was breaking up, I elbowed my way to the front and confronted him in front of dozens of reporters. "I find your comments insulting and I would ask that you apologize," I said. The minister stepped back, took a breath and quickly apologized. He went on to say he thought I was a fine member of Parliament.

That ended the matter as far as I was concerned. Unfortunately some Tories didn't see it that way. One of them, then party whip Chuck Cook, came up to me in the Commons the next day with a warning. Some women in his riding were sending me a message, so I should be ready for them, he said. Thanking him for the tip, I walked outside the House and was confronted by a clown bearing a giant helium-filled balloon and singing 'Baby Face'.

I was confused. The song itself seemed innocuous, and I didn't want to appear shrewish, so I hummed along. But a subsequent message was insulting: if I couldn't stand the heat of the House of Commons, I should stay out of the kitchen. My response was that

I love clowns and I love balloons, but I don't accept insults. When a member of Parliament is put down because she happens to be a woman, the insult applies to all women. I can take insults as well as I can dish them out, but the insults should be based on my ability, or lack of it, and not my gender.

Notwithstanding his apology, Crosbie recently used the word 'baby' when referring to me. I have written to the Speaker asking that certain sexist terms be ruled unparliamentary, but to date he has refrained from doing so. What does it say about the House of Commons when it's a breach of privilege to call anyone a scoundrel or liar, but acceptable to call a woman member titmouse or baby? I think we have some rule changing to do and I suspect it won't happen until we get greater numbers of women in the House.

Notwithstanding their party colours, when women members of Parliament work together, they can certainly be trailblazers. The equality committee looking into the charter changes was a case in point. While there are only 27 women in the House of Commons, four women were on this committee. The committee was charged with the responsibility of examining all current Canadian legislation to make sure that no law violates the charter. Where violations occur, the committee was to recommend changes to the law. The purpose of this was twofold: first, to make sure all Canadian laws were in conformity with the Canadian Constitution and the Charter of Rights; and second, to ensure that individuals whose rights were violated would not have to take the government to court. Rather, the government would redress inequalities with progressive legislation.

When the equality committee travelled across the country, it heard hundreds of recommendations for legislative change. Some were more controversial than others. Three of the most progressive recommendations included the abolition of mandatory retirement, women's full involvement in the Armed Forces, and the prohibition of discrimination against homosexuals. Notwithstanding the sensitive nature of these questions, the Conservative-dominated committee passed a unanimous report including recommendations in all three of these areas.

As soon as the the government reviewed the recommendations, the reality of equality was quite different. Speaking about women in the Armed Forces, Justice Minister John Crosbie assured the public that women would be able to compete equally for all jobs within the military except where certain operational risks were involved. 'Operational risks' were to be defined by the military command — the very group that had already fought so hard against equality for women in the military.

Similarly, Crosbie stated that sexual orientation should not be the basis for any discrimination in society. This was heartening news to minorities, who had faced dismissal from jobs and eviction from their homes simply because they were homosexuals. But instead of inserting a prohibition against discrimination on the basis of sexual orientation in the Canadian Human Rights Act, the minister claimed the Charter of Rights already provided protection. In fact, this assertion is absolutely false. A court action which sought to protect homosexuals against unfair job dismissal on the grounds that the classification of 'sex' in the Canadian Human Rights Act protected them, was thrown out because 'sex' legally refers only to gender. Hence, the minister's position that sexual orientation is covered by the Charter of Rights is groundless and has no legal force. Crosbie is forcing individuals and groups into the costly and uncomfortable position of having to sue through the courts because he lacks the political will to deal with sexual orientation in the Canadian Human Rights Act.

Recent reports indicate that some military leaders are conducting a survey of Armed Forces members, asking what they think about

171

sleeping next to a homosexual or working with a woman. Instead of implementing the equality provisions of the charter, the military seems bent on redefining equality on the basis of a public opinion poll.

The Conservatives have taken a positive step towards the abolition of mandatory retirement. Although the move applies only to those working in the federal public service and exempts private companies, it is a step in the right direction. Unfortunately, a close examination of the government's progressive legislation reveals that the only areas which saw real legislative change were those in which the courts had already taken the lead. Instead of showing real leadership in the area of equality, the justice minister chose only to follow the courts' initiative.

The government's actions on Mulroney's promises for employment equality for women and minorities are equally toothless and disappointing. The 'employment equity' act is almost insulting to women and minorities; its promises about employment equity do not survive scrutiny. The employment equity legislation sounds wonderful. All employers within certain categories will be required to file annual reports on their progress with employment equality or face fines up to $50,000. The fines make the legislation sound as though the government means business. But most companies are not covered by the legislation, and the federal government is itself exempted. Moreover, companies are only obliged to report their progress, not to act. The legislation makes no provision for an enforcement mechanism or for any kind of affirmative action.

Small wonder then, that the legislation prompted a demonstration on Parliament Hill. A group of frustrated disabled persons shouted, "Mulroney, baloney, your equity bill is phoney."

Women's groups remember too well what Mulroney promised during the women's debate. He promised to move immediately to redress the economic imbalance between men and women, by ensuring the implementation of contract compliance and guaranteeing that government departments would be covered by any future employment bill changes. In fact, the legislation makes no provision for compliance and all government departments are exempted from any change.

Whatever the party, the interests of women and minorities will remain on the back burner as long as the people in power are primarily male. That's why women must not only work for the candidate of their choice, but also commit themselves to seeking public office. Our political role must go beyond licking stamps and pouring coffee. We should make up the majority of candidates in the next federal election.

But that goal can only be met when women and political parties make our representation a priority. For women, that means being prepared to run the risk of being a candidate or working for someone who will best represent our point of view. For political parties, that means affirmative action and, yes, quotas to make sure that women have an equal chance to become candidates in winnable ridings. In the long run, with more women in Parliament, we will all be winners.

CHAPTER

19

A Day in the Life

Rule 19: Nobody ever claimed that politics is a picnic

So you've made it to the House on the Hill. Your strategy worked. Your campaign team delivered. Your party swept the country and you now find yourself a member of Parliament. What can you expect? How well does an outsider's view of the Hill actually match the real workings of Parliament and the responsibilities of the ordinary member?

Most Canadians are shocked if they visit Parliament when question period is not in progress. They look around and see only a scattering of members in the House — maybe 25 out of a possible 282. Even the few who are in the House seem to be doing almost anything other than listening to debates. Some are reading newspapers or getting caught up on correspondence. Others are chatting to their neighbours or talking to the only minister present in the House. For those who don't understand the system, there appears to be an almost total disregard for parliamentary debate. What most Canadians don't realize is that the real business of politics usually occurs outside the House. By the time a government policy becomes a bill — particularly when the government holds a ma-

174

jority — positions have hardened, and most members are there to uphold the views of their party, not to convince other members to change their minds. The wheeling and dealing usually occurs outside, away from the television cameras.

Even in committees, the possibility for changing government policy is limited. Ultimately, the cabinet is responsible for government policy. It meets in secret and is often not even accountable to its own caucus. This is particularly true in majority governments. A certain complacency sets in, when the cabinet realizes that it can simply ignore the opposition and whip the government backbenchers into line. For backbenchers, toeing the cabinet line may mean securing a coveted promotion — perhaps becoming a parliamentary secretary or even a cabinet minister.

Those of us in opposition have to be realistic about our ability to affect government policy, even with the recent changes in parliamentary rules. Ideally we would review cabinet decisions in much the same way that our American congressional cousins can. Unfortunately, parliamentary committees are not in a position to exercise real power. The cabinet is the final arbiter of government action. Majority governments effectively block the opposition parties from real involvement in the decision-making process. For these reasons, statements about the newfound power of the private member ring very hollow indeed.

The first private member's bill after the parliamentary committee reforms were introduced was a case in point. The issue in question was a government decision to include a pension as income for the purpose of deciding eligibility for Unemployment Insurance. If you were collecting a small pension from a previous job, you could be barred from receiving Unemployment Insurance even though you had to pay into the insurance scheme when you were working.

As soon as the changes were announced, 34,000 Canadians lost their UI benefits or had them reduced. Many of those affected were widows or retired Army personnel. Very few were living in luxury. Some people were forced to sell their homes because they had made retirement plans based on previous entitlement to Un-employment Insurance.

It seemed the perfect vehicle for a private members' vote — one which could register opposition to a government policy without causing the fall of the government. The debate inside and outside the House was stormy. But during private members' hour, not a single government member broke ranks to speak out against the policy that was hurting thousands of Canadians. Likewise, the private members' vote revealed that we were not acting as private members at all. Each party voted along party lines, and Conser-vatives who bitterly opposed the move merely absented themselves from the vote. Only one Conservative member actually voted against the government's proposed changes, even though dozens had spoken out against them in their home ridings. Parliamentary reform made no difference at all.

Perhaps the notion of a Parliament where each member is free to vote on a given issue would have as many drawbacks as advan-tages. Do we really want to replace our parliamentary system with the kind of government which has evolved in the United States? Consider the problems. Each congressman is assessed on the basis of a sort of scorecard of pluses and minuses for every vote taken in the Congress. An individual congressman who finds him or herself under attack by a particular political action committee is singled out for million-dollar ad campaigns designed to guarantee defeat. Such groups may serve a particular interest but not the public good. In effect, American politicians are held hostage; po-litical action committees control millions of dollars and will fund or destroy a congressman depending on their pet issue. The National

Riflemen's Association has such a stranglehold that the US Congress recently relaxed gun control laws in spite of well-organized and vocal opposition from law enforcement agencies and individual policemen. Perhaps with all its warts our system is a better one.

The collectivity of the party system in parliamentary democracy allows the public to assess whether government is working or not, and if not, where the blame should be apportioned. Individual members may collect plaudits or knocks, but in the end the collective judgement of political parties and of cabinet determine directions for our country. To suggest that this responsibility can be partitioned among individual members is to misunderstand the very basis of parliamentary democracy. The prime minister and the cabinet are ultimately responsible. They will make or break their government. While the individual member can remind them of their priorities, only they ultimately have the power to effect political change.

That is not to say the ordinary member has no role at all, but certainly that role must be seen in its context. As an opposition member, my business is to remind the government of its promises and objectives. I do this through committees, question period, speeches in the House of Commons and, above all, through the community.

Consider a day in the life of an ordinary member. Besides your time in the House, you may sit on any of almost 30 committees which examine everything from the services available to individual members to the human rights violations cited by the United Nations.

I am vice-chairman of the standing committee on human rights and also a substitute member on several other committees, including the committee on employment, labour and immigration. That means I meet in committee each week to examine issues ranging from human rights to various labour issues. The human rights committee was formed in response to recommendations on parliamentary reform. Since the committee is new we can carve out our own niche. The issues in international human rights are wide-ranging and often poorly understood. We enter the field not as experts but as parliamentarians who may have an individual interest in human rights. To suggest that we have the right to examine human rights violations in countries like South Africa and South Korea confers on us a serious responsibility. After all, there are experts in the field who are in a far better position to analyze the world situation than we are. But while we may call on these experts for guidance, it's up to parliamentarians to actually make the recommendations and apply political pressure.

Earlier this year, as vice-chairman of the human rights committee, I moved a motion calling on the Canadian government to impose complete economic sanctions on the pro-apartheid government of South Africa. To my surprise, the committee agreed to consider the resolution at a series of public hearings during the summer recess. While the hearings themselves cannot force the Canadian government's hand, that effort, combined with international events, helps to call the government's bluff. The hearings certainly played only a small part in mobilizing public opinion, but they may help to force the Canadian government into further action. Governments move slowly but you can't allow frustration to immobilize initiatives. Two steps forward one step back. That is what democracy is all about.

Like many professions, politics can appear glamorous if you're on the outside looking in; the pop of the flashbulbs, the parties at the National Art Centre that you see on television, the power, and the sense of being at the centre of things. But nothing is free: there is a heavy cost in emotional effort and time.

Each riding in Canada has its own set of problems and its own constituency complaints. But we all have one thing in common: people *do* look to their politicians to solve problems; national, local and individual. In many ways, Canadians have a schizophrenic view of our elected officials. On one hand, most people dismiss politicians as being crooks — power-hungry manipulators with their hands in the till, out for what they can get. On the other hand, we place impossible demands on our elected officials. Lower the deficit, reduce inflation, reduce unemployment, and while you're at it, do you think you could get my son a job? Quite clearly, individual politicians have no more say over the state of the world economy than the average citizen. But somehow we look up to our civic and national leaders to deliver the answers, all the while knowing that they can't.

How does this all add up? No, we shouldn't abolish the democratic process — it works reasonably well and is better than the alternatives. But we should understand the limitations of every leader, every party and every government. It is our job in opposition to point out where the government is going wrong, but those of us who have never run a government must face an underlying question: would we be any better?

We aren't going to find out whether we would be any better unless we get elected. And that means being on the hustings all the time. Organization is not restricted only to your own riding and your own community. If you believe in your party and the job that volunteers across the country are trying to do, then you must support them by travelling to political events in the far corners of Canada. Since there are so few of us in caucus, each of us must take on more of the workload.

In the 39-member Liberal caucus, our responsibility extends far beyond our individual ridings. I regularly travel to other parts of the country to spread the message of Liberalism. During our first eighteen months in opposition, I visited every province and territory except Saskatchewan and the Yukon. I will probably visit them before the year is out.

In addition we are called to talk about Liberalism and party policy to non-political groups and organizations. This means more travel and more preparation to ensure that the Liberal message is getting out.

The government has the cabinet, Parliament and the civil service to carry out its political agenda. The opposition parties must rely on the press and personal appearances to counterbalance this enormous weight. Not that the civil service is selling the Conservative message, but its job is to carry out the political wishes of the governing party. For example, consider privatization. The Mulroney government's philosophy is also part of the government agenda, and thousands of civil servants are responsible for implementing the government's policy. Compare that to the ten full-time researchers in the federal Liberal caucus and the four or five employees teamed with each Liberal member of Parliament. The odds against us are overwhelming; we must work that much harder.

The caucus and the party organization cooperate to develop policy which reflects the views of the majority of members. The process involves local regional policy conferences and provincial and national conventions on issues as varied as free trade and the guaranteed annual income.

The party has to listen not only to its members, but also to others in the community with innovative ideas, people who may share the Liberal philosophy without being card-carrying party members. As MPs we help to build policy in the caucus and the party as a whole. We might, for example, join workshops and seminars, writing papers and generally stimulating discussions in our area of expertise. Part of my job as the Liberal chairman for social policy is to form a network of contacts across the country, with the help of party presidents, which will help us rapidly learn what is happening in the field. It will also allow us to get our social policy message out quickly and effectively.

We have to communicate with the people of Canada, not only to get elected, but also to keep our sanity. The sense of unreality on the Hill taints our views of what is happening across the country. Ottawa is a tidy, prosperous city. The poverty here (and it does exist) is all but invisible. The city's preoccupations are power, politics and status. It's very easy to forget that the rest of Canada lives very differently. Not all Canadian families — not even all Ottawa families — have two civil-service incomes. The capital has been accused of being an ivory tower, and the accusations are largely true. The closer you get to Parliament, the quicker unreality sets in.

I noticed the difference the first day I walked into the House of Commons. Everything was "yes sir", "no sir", "yes ma'am", "no ma'am". Employees on the Hill learn very quickly that members of Parliament are their bosses, and what a member wants, he or she gets. If you need a message taken or a tour of the Parliament Buildings organized, they are only too happy to oblige. Anything that can make your life easier is their responsibility.

Having come from Queen's Park, I found the difference startling. In the Ontario legislature, after 40 years in opposition, we were almost treated as nuisances, as though our work interfered with the smooth running of government, and the less we said and did the better. This held true whether you wanted basic information or a briefing on a new government programme or policy. When I got to Ottawa, it was the exact opposite. As soon as I was appointed labour and housing critic, the deputy minister and his staff were available for briefings on all the workings of the department. The president of the Canada Mortgage and Housing Corporation agreed to meet with me immediately and outline government initiatives in housing programmes. The Library of Parliament was most helpful and would pull out studies in any area I wished, whether on the effects of polling on political parties or the cost of universal daycare. Wherever I went, I was amazed by the openness, the willingness to help. The staff seemed to feel that Parliament Hill was there for each parliamentarian, not just for the government in power.

It was a pleasant contrast to the situation in Toronto. But after a while, you begin to take this sort of power for granted. We work daily in a situation where people almost jump to their feet when we snap our fingers. Look at the House of Commons pages. These university students continue their studies while carrying a full work-load on the Hill. While they are on House duty, it is their job to respond to the wishes of any member of Parliament. That may involve anything from delivering a message or answering a phone, to picking up a chocolate bar for a member who can't leave the chamber. They perform their jobs cheerfully and quickly. They never complain or object — at least not in our hearing. Soon we come to expect this service. It's altogether too easy to become arrogant.

It's not just the Hill, either. Ottawa is a government town. When you go to the grocery store or the local watering hole, people recognize you. They may say hello and be friendly or they may only stare in curiosity. You are living in a goldfish bowl where public attention becomes a fact of life.

Last winter I flew out to Winnipeg and barely made the flight because of some ticket problems. When I arrived on the aircraft, I tried to jam my heavy sheepskin coat in the overhead bin. The bin was already too full so I moved my coat to the bin behind my seat. I had trouble closing that one too, so I left it open, hoping that the flight attendant might be able to accomplish what I couldn't. A week later, I received a telephone call from the local newspaper.

Someone who had been on the flight with me had called the newspaper to complain about my rudeness in not closing the bin.

Wherever you go, Big Brother is watching you. Obviously that's one of the prices you pay for being in politics. But there's a still higher price. Politicians get hooked on fame — they're addicts. What happens if you are defeated? If you need public recognition to be validated as a person, then a defeat or a loss of standing is especially crushing. It clobbers your ego.

That's why I try to keep the Ottawa scene in perspective. You're a hero today and a bum tomorrow. You must constantly remind yourself of the reasons you came to Ottawa. Don't be drawn in by the political flavour of the town. Ottawa is a politician's dream; it's where the action is. You can sense it in the air. I can feel it every day I walk up that long Hill to my office in the main Parliament building. This is where decisions involving the very future of our country are made. But it is also the town of broken dreams and marriages, of private lives marked by sacrifices and difficulty. It is a town where you can lose everything if you allow yourself to. You can succumb to the city's seduction, or you can hold on to your integrity and try to make a difference, sometimes as an individual member but more often as part of a team. Your chance to make changes only exists as long as you realize that your *raison d'être* is not the chauffeur-driven limousine or the ministerial perquisites that go with power, but making life a little more liveable for others, giving young people a little more hope, making the country a little more productive. Perhaps the lessons of power can best be learned in opposition. One individual member cannot move mountains. But if you stick together and keep your goals in sight, anything is possible.

All this takes much time, effort and organizational skill. Luckily we don't work alone. I have one staffer, Danielle May, who specializes in social policy, another, Gordon Douglas, in economic and trade issues and a third, Barry Strader who spends much more than an eight-hour day keeping me organized and providing constituency followup on Parliament Hill. I also have two riding as-sistants, Anne-Marie Blanche and Linda Kotsopoulos, who deal on a daily one-to-one basis with people who come to their member of Parliament seeking advice about a problem. My total staff budget is about $100,000 — not nearly enough to pay staffers what they deserve. On average, they work ten- to twelve-hour days.

In most cases, they are also highly political in their own right. Some members of Parliament forbid their staff to have any extra-curricular political involvement. But I believe that no one works for a politician simply for the money. One's staff has a social conscience too, and a political vision which can't be turned off when the working day ends. I encourage my staffers to get involved in local and provincial election campaigns — even in internal campaigns for various party positions. Nothing would make me happier than to someday see one of them leave my office to seek political office. They work hard, the job is stimulating and, like me, they are political animals. The addiction, once formed, is permanent. But the pay is poor, the hours are long and the degree of burnout in working for a member of Parliament is very high. They too must learn to set limits.

There's no doubt about it, members of Parliament do earn their salaries. It's a continual struggle to keep up with the workload, to handle committees, question period, and constituency matters, to field questions as they arise, to learn the issues as quickly and thoroughly as possible. It's a struggle of another sort to keep your internal balance — not to forget what real life is like.

I don't want to sound self-pitying. It should be obvious by now that I love politics and find it enormously rewarding. Otherwise why would I try so hard to draw other women into the political arena? The workload, like the risk, is enormous, although so are the benefits. But don't take my word for it.

20

You've Got a Long Way to Go

Rule 20: So don't forget your compass

I was sitting at home one night after a bad day in the House of Commons, feeling miserable and asking myself all the wrong questions. It just happened to be one of those days. An impromptu weekend remark by my friend, John Nunziata, had reopened all the wounds remaining from the leadership question. John had mentioned that he felt the leadership review process was divisive and he preferred going straight to a leadership convention. Naturally the press picked up on the latter part of his statement. "Liberal MP calls for leadership convention," the headlines read. I felt depressed because I didn't want the party to be drawn into another discussion on the leadership. I also felt miserable because, at a press gallery dinner, the prime minister had excelled and my own leader's performance could only be kindly described as short of brilliant. These little events don't make or break a political career. But sometimes they can be very hard to take.

Then the phone rang. A reporter from the Canadian Press wanted my reaction to the Prince Edward Island election. "What was the result?" I asked with trepidation. A Liberal landslide. My depression vanished. Three Liberal premiers in three elections since Brian

Mulroney became prime minister! Two steps forward, one back, and another three forward.

In politics, as in other professions, it is important to set your sights on both the short-term and long-term goals. The short-term may divert your attention from time to time, but if you keep the long-term goals in sight then no individual setback will permanently stymie you.

Not that it comes easily. Setting limits is probably one of the most difficult things in a politician's life. It's not easy to say no, particularly because one of the forces that draws people into politics is the need for recognition. If a local organization in Newfoundland desperately needs me for a speaking engagement, I am flattered. I automatically want to say yes. But if I say yes to all the people, all of the time, I will have no time left for myself, my husband and family. Perhaps this is one of the greatest impediments to a woman's career in politics. You need time — to be a wife, a mother, yourself, and a politician. The only way to make time stretch in all directions is to set your priorities and stick to them.

When Pierre Trudeau was prime minister, he always reserved Sunday for his family. A devoted father, he decided early on that Sundays were strictly for his children. But if your constituency is thousands of kilometres from Ottawa, it takes all of Sunday just to get back to Ottawa in time for the weekly routine to begin again on Monday.

I have been lucky in one respect. I started young; when I have children at least I will not have to uproot them. When I married, my husband chose to move to Ottawa. He was immigrating to Canada and we both felt that it would be easier to see each other during the week, and set weekends aside for constituency work.

As for a family, the children will be with both of us at least five days a week.

Most men enter the political arena when their children are teenagers. It is simply impossible to ask the whole family to pick up and move to Ottawa, particularly if the children are in local schools. Usually the wife stays home and the husband returns on weekends. But even this time cannot be totally devoted to the family, since he also has his constituency work. It can be a very lonely life all around. Lonely for the wife, who feels abandoned all week as her husband heads off to Ottawa and saddles her with total responsibility for the children. And lonely for the husband, who finds himself staring at the four walls of a tiny apartment during the four or five nights that he must spend away from home every week.

In spite of its superficial glamour, a political life can be an unhappy, even a dangerous, one. The MP living in Ottawa and separated from his family during the week can either drown himself in his work or find other outlets for the inevitable void. Since those outlets can include alcohol and infidelity, it's no wonder that politics ranks very high on the scale of professions vulnerable to marriage breakdown.

The politician isn't the only one who suffers. If the spouse does not enjoy politics, she can feel trapped in a lifestyle not of her choosing. Politics isn't the kind of job you can leave at 5 pm. It's with you and your family on weekends when a constituent calls to complain about a problem. It is with you on Saturday night when you make social calls in your riding. That added stress on a spouse may do more damage than the physical separation. The ideal solution is either to get involved at a young age, when you can move the family to Ottawa if necessary, or to wait until your family is grown so that you and your spouse can have more free time.

But timing is not always of our own choosing. Many women simply despair of a political career because the logistics of raising a family, running a home and working at such a demanding oc-

187

cupation are overwhelming. Obviously, to succeed at all three, you must have a very supportive spouse. And you have to decide which comes first. When all is said and done, your family will be with you long after politics has passed, so they must come first. But help is available. As a member of Parliament, your financial position is much easier than that of the average working family. You can afford top-quality child care because your salary puts you in the top 10 per cent of the population. The House of Commons has a daycare programme called Children on the Hill for children aged two and a half and up. While most of the children are drawn from the families of the thousands of employees who work as the support staff to Parliament, members can also enter their children in the programme. Before that age, you're faced with the perennial problem of adequate daycare multiplied tenfold by your own hectic schedule. No one can deny that the dual role of mother and member is not an easy one. Sure the supports may be there. You may have a terrific husband and the greatest network in the world. But until you have stayed up all night to nurse a kid with colic or coped with a family epidemic of chicken pox in mid-election, you can't know whether you can manage everything.

I have to speak as an amateur, on the outside looking in. I certainly hope to combine the joys of parenthood and politics, but I can't know whether I can manage both until I try. I do think that any woman who wants to combine the two must be prepared early on to set her priorities and make sure they are realistic. You must accept that you won't be the best housekeeper on the block, but maybe you can afford a housekeeper. You won't be able to provide freshly baked cookies. But the children may gain in other ways. They will have a chance to see equality in action. They will experience in a direct way the joys and sacrifices involved in your work as an elected representative. They will have a chance to understand how democracy works, by watching and helping you as you work your way through the painful process of learning the ropes, whether on city council or at the provincial or federal level. And your family will share the collective challenge of organizing and mobilizing a whole community, at election time or in between.

There are risks involved to both you and your family. As a daughter of a politician I know the risks well. I can tell you there are times when you feel shortchanged because you have to share a parent with the whole community.

Take my own family. My sister Brenda hates politics. She feels the public aspect of political life is insupportable. As a medical doctor, she is committed to public service, but she hates the idea of inhabiting a goldfish bowl. Despite her misgivings, she gets involved in all my campaigns and actually does a great job on the hustings. Although she disavows any other political involvement, her husband, David Smith, has become a staunch party worker. As a duo, Brenda and Dave ran my election day organization in the last campaign and Dave has stayed heavily involved in party work.

Another sister, Mary, loves politics. She got her feet wet again when I ran for the provincial leadership. She went on to become a member of the provincial executive and was the canvass organizer in the landslide provincial Liberal victory of Joan Smith (a city councillor who defeated then cabinet minister Gord Walker in what could only be described as a smashing upset). Mary's husband, Barry Sutherland, also got involved in my campaigns and is an executive member of the local riding association in London. In the last municipal election, Barry's whole family came out to help my mother get elected.

My brother Kevin is also a political animal. His interests extend beyond national boundaries, since his work as an economist has prompted him to study world political and economic systems and how they interrelate.

Each one drew something positive from politics, but each one also carries the scars of a childhood where dad wasn't always around. Other political families probably have similar stories. Is it all worth the cost? I think so. Am I prepared to bring up my children as I was brought up? Yes.

My long-term goals are modest. I don't believe that any individual can set the city, the country or the world on fire, but I do believe that I can play a small role in helping make Canada a better place to live. I believe that we must work inside the existing political process if we are to effect social change. Not that the system is perfect, nor can any political party claim authorship for all positive social change. But it's the only system we've got and it's better than any other I know of. It's up to us to make it work.

The people must lead the way, notwithstanding Ottawa's belief that politicians and the press can shape popular opinion. Some examples: tax reform was only an idea in the minds of a couple of members when the ordinary Canadian began to demand it. A national, accessible health care system which puts the rich, the poor, the old and the young on the same footing will never survive unless we all want it. Early childhood education? Accessible day-care? These will only be feminist rallying cries unless families start to demand them. Politicians cannot always lead public opinion. They can reinforce the demand in society for changes that will create a more equal climate for the growth of each individual. But they are nothing without the support of the people.

My political career will not last long. I don't intend to stay in politics for a lifetime. I understand the limitations of what anyone can achieve. But I also hope that when I leave the federal scene, the opportunity for other women to enter the House of Commons will be greater. Why do I want this? I am not interested in electing women merely for the sake of swelling our numbers in the House. But I believe fundamentally that women have different perspectives to bring to our country. The only way we will see a democratic reflection of those perspectives is to send more women to the House of Commons.

Women see the need for our national health care system most clearly. Because we bear and raise children, and since we outlive men, women are the greatest users of the system. We see the effects of a national education policy with public access for all. And in our daily lives, we experience first hand the benefits of our way of life — a lower crime rate, less personal violence, clean and lively cities.

If you are a woman, the road to the House is not an easy one. You will have to fight like a man — to be forceful, aggressive, and to the point. You can't afford to pull your punches. You are breaking into a man's game at a time when many men are struggling to maintain their hold on the country's power structures.

But you should not enter into this man's world just for the sake of gaining power. After all, if you replace one power-hungry politician with another, what have you achieved? You are bringing a unique perspective, a woman's perspective, and this can add much to the political landscape.

Every human being longs for a chance to dream, to make a city, a country, a world, a little better for his or her children. Politics can help us move toward that dream. But if it is truly a shared dream, we must all — rich and poor, men and women — have an equal stake in the political process. By remaining on the outside looking in, we lose the chance to build the dream, to make sure it reflects our interests and our values.

Above all, and this may sound stereotyped, you should think of the children. Maybe it's about time our politicians thought more about them, and about their welfare; especially when we realize that almost 20 per cent of Canadian children are living in poverty. Perhaps it is time we considered them when we learn that thousands of mothers are being forced onto welfare, while society permits fathers to walk away from their responsibilities for wife and child support. When the federal government announced that there was no consensus on the issue of daycare, and that the only help they could give to the growing number of latchkey kids was to start another task force, were they thinking of the children? When the Canadian government refused to reintroduce a clause into the North Atlantic Treaty Organization agreement to guarantee that no nuclear weapons would be allowed on Canadian soil, it wasn't thinking about the children.

Maybe we've been led too long by 'masculine' ideals of conquest and aggression rather than by 'feminine' urges to nurture and protect. Each of us, man and women, has aspects of both. But in the political process as in society at large, we have allowed those aggressive, overpowering instincts to suppress the attributes of harmony and growth. Those masculine qualities are needed. But they must be balanced by benevolence and cooperation, traditional female characteristics which have been so absent from political life.

Women are moving forward, in politics and in life. "You've come a long way, baby," as the saying goes. But until all of us are 'nobody's babies', we won't have come nearly far enough.

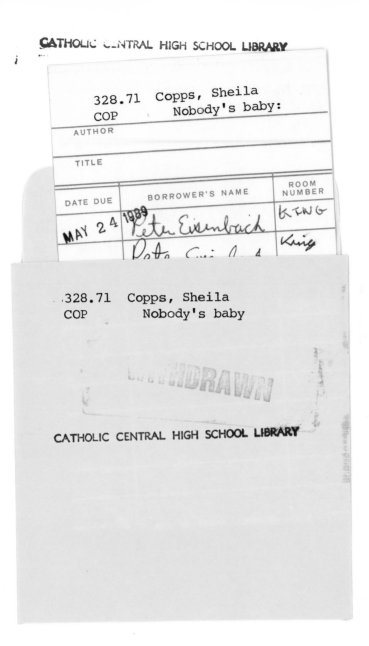